STOP
BEING A
SUPER
CHICKEN

The Importance of Building Relationships
at Work and at Home

LANA T. BAVLE, *MA, CEC, RMA*

 FriesenPress

One Printers Way
Altona, MB R0G 0B0
Canada

www.friesenpress.com

ISBN
978-1-03-919830-2 (Hardcover)
978-1-03-919829-6 (Paperback)
978-1-03-919831-9 (eBook)

1. BUSINESS & ECONOMICS, LEADERSHIP

Distributed to the trade by The Ingram Book Company

Table of Contents

"To tell. To use the act of breathing to shape air into sounds that take on the context of language that lifts and transports those who hear it, takes them beyond what they think and know and feel and empowers them to think and feel and know even more. We're all storytellers, really. That's what we do. That is our power as human beings. Not to tell people how to think and feel and therefore know – but through our stories allow them to discover questions within themselves. Turn off your TV and your devices and talk to each other. Share stories. Be joined, transported and transformed."

- Richard Wagamese

Introduction

In the summer of 2022, I was asked by a former colleague to give a presentation at a pre-conference workshop for her board of directors. The only guidelines she gave me were that I had about forty-five minutes and the presentation needed to focus on professional development. She had no budget to provide me with an honorarium; however, she would happily endorse my business, LTB Leadership, so I said yes. I sat on this for a few months without knowing exactly where I wanted to go and then started searching for ideas.

During this time, one my colleagues spoke of a TED Talk video called 'Forget the pecking order at work' (From here on in referred to as 'Super Chickens'). I found it, watched it, and loved it. It truly inspired me. I have included a link to the video in the reference section at the end of this book.

In the video, Margaret Heffernan speaks about how an evolutionary biologist at Purdue University, William Muir, studied chickens as he was interested in productivity. He chose chickens because it was easy to measure their productivity: you simply had to count how many eggs they laid. She shares that Muir devised an experiment by selecting an average flock of chickens and leaving them alone for six generations. Then, he established a second group of chickens by choosing high egg layers and putting them together as a super flock.

After six generations, he noticed a few things. The first flock of average chickens was doing just fine, but with the second group, only three had survived. This was because the only way the super chickens could succeed was to suppress the productivity of the others; therefore, all but three were pecked to death. She goes on to say that it is not the IQs of the individuals that matter. It's how they collaborate as a group, their connectedness and inclusion. Heffernan ended the TED Talk by saying she realized how much more we could give each other if we stopped trying to be super chickens.

Jackpot! I found the idea for my presentation! I watched the video numerous times and pulled out some themes I wanted to explore in my presentation. The pieces I picked out were positivity, motivation, resilience, competition, team building, productivity, community, psychological safety, relationship intelligence, and bringing out the best in ourselves and others.

To give you some of my background, I had recently retired from a fifteen-year career as Chief Administrative Officer (CAO) for municipal government in Southwest Saskatchewan. I then did a short stint in sales, selling software I had used in the office for a decade. As a side note, I loved this software, the company, the team, and the culture. It was one of my favourite positions over three decades of being in the workforce. Unfortunately, a merger/acquisition created an environment with no psychological safety, no clear leadership, and no inclusion, so I decided there was no better time to "leap" and see if the net would appear. After that experience, I decided to do what I love: helping people learn, grow, and build better relationships. Hence, I decided to focus my attention full-time on consulting and launching my own consulting firm, LTB Leadership, in early 2022.

Being part of a merger/acquisition where the key focus was on acquiring many companies and making money was also a gift because I learnt firsthand about what working for a company with no psychological safety, poor leadership, terrible culture, and an extremely high turnover rate was like. This experience was an excellent opportunity to grow, build resilience, and add more tools to my practice.

I presented the webinar to the pre-conference group, which went swimmingly. There were two of us presenting that morning, and without having had a conversation with each other, our two presentations went hand in hand beautifully. A rich conversation resulted in a strong desire for me to know and do more. Later that month, I visited a friend who is also a mentor to me, someone I respect and who was a successful business owner. He said to me, "LB, you need to write a book. I don't care what you write a book on; just write a book." I put the wheels into motion. I love the themes in the Super Chickens presentation, and decided a written version would be an asset to anyone who wants to bring more success to their organization. I would write a book that focused on the importance of team building and relationships.

This book is full of my own experiences shared through stories. I have a rule in my life of practicing simplicity. It is one of my three core values. In case you were wondering, the other two are honesty and fairness. I approach everything in life with simplicity, so there are no fancy words, complex theories, or confusing ideas in this book, only simple stories and experiences to share what I know to be true at this point in my journey. There are three parts to this short book. Part One speaks to you as individuals and has a focus on self. Part Two speaks more to teams and has a focus on self with others. And finally, Part Three speaks more to organizations themselves and how to increase their effectiveness.

In my consulting practice, I offer several services. I am an executive coach, a team building and leadership development workshop facilitator, and a mentor for new entrepreneurs and acting administrators in Saskatchewan municipal government. I also offer personal and professional development training through Lunch and Learn workshops, have a program for enhancing organizational effectiveness, and work with municipalities and their administration to set strategic directions. I am constantly developing new programs and services and am now writing a book.

This book has chapters sharing the themes I pulled from the TED Talk. (Did you know that TED stands for "Technology, Entertainment, Design," the media organization that posts talks online?) At the end of each chapter are Hen's House Highlights, which summarize the chapter's key points.

I am writing this book from my heart, knowing that what I have to share may help others understand that being a super chicken is not what is needed in today's organizations. We need to learn how to communicate better and build stronger relationships. These ideas or themes in this book will apply to you and your relationships both at work and at home. And finally, I use the term folks throughout the book as I feel that that term is all-inclusive, and it is important to me to be respectful of everyone, their cultures, and their histories.

As a final note, before we move into part one, I want to reiterate I am writing this book from my heart and sharing stories with you to make the content more relatable. I hope you take away at least one or two nuggets, even if it is only to use more water when flushing a camper toilet (go on... keep reading... you know you wanna).

Here we go! Let's explore the first part of this book, starting with positivity and motivation.

PART ONE

CHAPTER 1
Positivity & Motivation

In the Super Chickens video, Heffernan said that what motivates people is the bonds, loyalty, and trust they develop between each other. To build those relationships, there needs to be interaction. If you are a leader in your organization, it is your responsibility to break down the silos (if there are any) and create safe spaces for your teams to work together, solve issues, brainstorm, and create.

Provide psychological safety and ensure your folks know how to communicate effectively, especially in challenging situations of opposition or conflict. Psychological safety is the ability to show and employ oneself without fear of negative self-image, status, or career consequences. It is the ability to establish and engage oneself without fear of negative results. We will explore psychological safety in greater detail in Chapter Seven.

I love the Cherokee Indian legend of the two wolves. For those unfamiliar with it, this is what it says:

> One evening, an old Cherokee man told his grandson about a battle that goes on inside a person.
>
> "That battle is between two wolves who live inside us all," the grandfather said. "One wolf is evil. It is anger, envy, jealousy, sorrow, regret, greed, arrogance, self-pity, guilt, resentment, inferiority, lies, pride, superiority, and ego. The other is good. It is joy, peace, love, hope, serenity, humility, kindness, benevolence, empathy, generosity, truth, compassion, and faith."
>
> The grandson thought about it for a minute and then asked his grandfather: "Which one wins?"
>
> The old Cherokee told his grandson the answer was simple: "The one you feed."

I share this legend as it shows the importance of how we feed ourselves, what we tell ourselves, and how we do have control over our choices. Positivity is a choice and is the topic I will focus on in this chapter. I will show you how positivity and an appreciative mindset can help individuals, teams, and organizations thrive.

The Power of Positivity

The power of positivity is a motivational aid. By this, I mean that practicing an appreciative or positive lifestyle and having the same mindset, will motivate individuals to accomplish and be more.

Twenty years ago, I read an impactful fable where the main character had to commit to getting up an hour earlier for twenty-eight days. The way I remember it is that he had the choice of what he could do with this extra hour. He could set goals, exercise, read, journal, meditate, or pick a project where he could be creative. I played with this idea when I finished reading the book. Sometimes I walked for the whole hour. Sometimes I read for an entire hour. Sometimes I did a combination of the other options. Where I settled, and have never stopped, is with my current morning routine.

My morning routine consists of getting up, making my coffee, and then sitting down to read for at least twenty minutes. Last year I read thirty-two books by doing this (with maybe some extra reading on the weekends). Imagine all I learnt and the adventures I went on last year. In the morning, when I am done reading, I journal for ten to fifteen minutes. I use this time to self-coach, create to-do lists, work through issues, record life happenings, and set intentions.

Once I am done reading and journaling, I practice yoga. Usually, I do a ten-minute video that I found on YouTube. I have been doing these ten-minute yoga practices every day for two and a half years, and let me tell you, it makes a huge difference in my flexibility and balance—mentally, emotionally, and physically. Once I am done with these three things, I feel balanced, grounded, and ready to start my day. It helps me to live my life with intention and purpose. I practice self-care before diving into what sometimes is a hectic day.

I suggest that you play with this morning routine concept. See what feels right for you. And know that it can change over time. For me, it is so exciting to learn, grow, and take care of myself. I hope you find something you are excited about that will bring more positivity into your life. You might choose to paint, write poetry, lift weights, hike, bike, or whatever it is that puts you in the best space to tackle the day and have a positive mindset to be your most productive self.

Charles R. Swindoll said, "Life is 10% what happens to us and 90% how we react to it." We always have a choice about how to deal with what life throws at us. We can accept what is happening and gracefully (or not so gracefully, but still) move through it, or we can stomp our feet and be angry and upset, which is never a good use of our time or our life. I have a couple of stories I will share with you in the next chapter on resilience that will show how we can approach challenges in a positive way, helping us to gently navigate through difficult situations.

Practicing Positivity

Gratitude is another important activity and habit; one that I practice every day.

> *It's difficult not to be positive when you are grateful for what you have, where you are, and who you have in your life.*

Life is a gift that can be short and is so precious. We need to be respectful of that every day. It can be taken away from us at any time. Here are some ways that you can practice gratitude.

I find that writing things down makes them more concrete. This applies to setting goals as well as practicing gratitude. It's a great exercise to make a list of what you are grateful for at the end of the day. If you like, you can even purchase a gratitude journal. However, you can also use an ordinary journal or notebook. What you put in the journal is more important than what the journal is.

For many years, I practiced this, writing down the things I was grateful for every day. In the last few years, I have changed my practice and mentally summarize all I am grateful for in my day as I drift off to sleep. It is much more beneficial to go to sleep thinking of what you are grateful for rather than focusing on what went wrong or what you didn't do or get done. Being grateful is a simple positive habit to practice that has excellent results.

If this isn't your cup of tea, Sheryl Sandberg wrote a book called *Option B: Facing Adversity, Building Resilience, and Finding Joy*. In it, she explains that her list was not one of gratitude but more so what she had done well that day. Either of these practices aims to promote positivity, focus on the good rather than the bad, and have an appreciative mindset.

Setting intentions is another practice for positivity. I practice setting intentions in a few different ways. One thing I always do when I get in my car and start driving is say to myself: "Safe travels." I feel more grounded because I am setting the intention that I am going to have a safe trip, and it helps me to be a safer driver and more aware. It helps me remember to pay attention to the road and the others I share it with.

In all my training sessions, whether it be a Lunch & Learn workshop that I facilitate, or a team building or leadership development workshop, I do a reading, almost always from the book *Embers* by Richard Wagamese (one of my favourite authors), again to set the intention for the time I am sharing with others. If you have not read any of his books, I highly recommend you pick one up. *Embers: One Ojibway's Meditations* is a great book.

Each morning, when I finish journaling, I always throw a one-liner in at the end where I set my intention for the day. Most of the time, it is simply something like "It is going to be a great day" or "It is going to be a productive day." Sometimes, on the weekend, I intend to have a gentle day, especially after a big week at work when I need to practice some self-care, rejuvenate, and prepare for the following week. Setting intentions is a way of putting what you want out into the universe; in my experience, by setting my intention at the start of the day I find that that same intention/energy comes back to me.

Another thing you can do to increase your positivity is read or listen to something uplifting, something that will grow your mind or spirit. There are so many great books to feed your mind with. One of the most impactful books I read was *The Power of Now* by Eckhart Tolle. (I read it almost twenty years ago.) The message in his book is that if you fret about the past and worry about the future, you will miss out on what is happening and opening up for you, right here, right now. We don't know what the future holds for us. The best we can do is live the heck out of today in case there is no tomorrow. If you are not happy, make some changes because life is just too short to be unhappy.

Some of my other favourite authors include Robin Sharma and Brené Brown. Sharma often writes fables to share information with us about living a more intentional

STOP BEING A SUPER CHICKEN

and positive life. Brené Brown writes all about self-awareness and self-care. She helps us to understand ourselves
and others better. And then, of course, there is Patrick
Lencioni. He writes terrific fables that assist us in leadership and business. If you don't like reading, listen to audio-
books or podcasts to feed your mind and soul.

Many other great authors and motivational speakers
can help us feel great, grow, and help others around us
grow as well. One of my favourite speakers I have listened
to for years is Les Brown. He talks about the importance of
being driven. He often says, "You gotta be hungry." Hungry
for knowledge, hungry to do more, hungry to be more (or
at least that's what I get from it). By filling your mind with
this information and positivity, you write your own story
instead of allowing life to write it for you.

I recently finished Hayley Wickenheiser's book
called *Over the Boards*. Hayley comes from Shaunavon,
Saskatchewan, where I lived before moving to Vancouver
Island in British Columbia. She is a former Canadian
female ice hockey player, resident physician, and assistant
general manager for the Toronto Maple Leafs. She was the
first woman to play full-time professional hockey in a position other than goalie.

In her book, she talks about staying focused and positive
and how it was tough to do that all the time. Sometimes
she just needed some time not to be positive and have a
bit of a freak-out session. She explains that when she needs
this, she sets a timer for twenty minutes and allows herself
that time to freak out, worry about every little thing going
on, and consider the crappy things happening. When the

twenty minutes are up, she puts all that stuff out of her mind and carries on with the day.

I decided to try this out one weekend. I had had a few bumps in the previous five weeks. (By a few, I mean six). Soon after that, I was faced with another bump that I struggled with. So, one Sunday morning, I decided to allow myself time to journal these bumps out, wallow in their crappiness, and see what would come about. Without me planning for it, this is what happened. I wrote out the seven challenges in list form that I had in the last five weeks, not really spending a bunch of time exploring each one of them, and it felt okay to do that. It didn't drag me down or bring up any real emotions. When I had nothing else negative to list, I automatically listed all the positive things that had happened in that same time frame. And fortunately, there were eleven positive things. It brought me peace to see that it wasn't all doom and gloom, and guess what? That's life. How interesting that even though more positive things were happening, I was still focusing on the negative. It's the same as when someone says something negative about us or something we have done; it doesn't matter if fifteen people give us compliments and support us; we tend to concentrate on that one negative thing.

It's okay to be realistic and acknowledge that things suck sometimes, but don't stay in that space any longer than you need to. I like Hayley's twenty-minute freak-out sessions and will use them if and when necessary. Likely, I will often find that there is more to be grateful for and there are more positive than negative things happening around me.

Appreciative Mindset and Appreciative Inquiry

One of my colleagues, Dr. Tom Weegar, spoke recently about appreciative inquiry at a college function in Northern Saskatchewan. He stated that appreciative inquiry is a collaborative strength-based approach to change in organizations and other human systems. He says that appreciative inquiry is a great way to engage groups of people in self-determined change.

I used an appreciative inquiry approach when I was completing my research for my master's degree. Appreciative Inquiry (AI) is a process that focuses on what is working rather than focusing on problems from the past. It focuses on who, what, and where we want to be. It concentrates on what we want more of rather than what we want less of. This is similar to *The Secret*, which suggests that we bring about what we think about. Dr. Kathy Bishop (2017) explains in her YouTube video on the MA Leadership Program that appreciative inquiry is "taking some type of action to effect some type of positive change in the world."

In my thesis (2020), I wrote, "Working collaboratively, looking for what is working well, and then finding ways to implement those same practices in the future is the essence of appreciative inquiry." We often hear about gratitude and positivity; they both have an appreciative perspective. I also wrote that "Appreciative inquiry is not only what we do for and with others, but also with ourselves."

Cooperrider and Whitney (2005) shared, "Human systems grow in the direction of what they persistently ask questions about, and this propensity is strongest and most sustainable when the means and ends of inquiry are positively correlated. The most important action a group can take to liberate the human spirit and consciously construct a better future is to make the positive core the common explicit property of all." Positiveness and appreciation or gratitude are two absolute musts in an appreciative process.

How to Motivate Your Team

When you treat your employees right, loyalty is likely to follow. Treating them right can look like planning events and activities that help your employees form bonds and build trust. Motivating your team is similar to increasing their productivity, which we explore in Chapter Five. Getting to know your team and what is important to them will help uncover ways to provide them with what they need to increase their motivation. Remember that motivation is not always about the money, although for some, it will be. Everyone can be motivated by something different.

One year, I was in wage negotiations with the municipality I was working for. One of the elected officials commented that the only thing that motivated employees was money. I remember sitting there thinking about it and finally challenged her on that statement. Money is not what motivated me. I acknowledged that I was very privileged and made enough money to cover my living expenses and then some. Money is essential to cover our basic needs, but after that, some folks are motivated by something entirely different.

After we have everything we need to live, motivation may be more about opportunities or ways of enjoying life. That year I negotiated an extra week's holiday rather than more money. I wanted opportunities to make memories and have experiences knowing that more money would not give me the fulfillment I was looking for.

It's important to know what we want in this life. Once we figure that out, we can focus on obtaining more of it. When it comes to our career, this can only happen if we share it with the organizations we work with. If you are lucky enough to work for an organization that values its employees, they will certainly do their best to provide you with what you desire, knowing that it will motivate you to do better and be more productive. Let's now explore the importance of resilience and how to build it.

Hen House Highlights
- A huge part of motivation revolves around our mindset and the relationships we build.
- Positivity and an appreciative mindset can help individuals, teams, and organizations thrive.
- We always have a choice on how to deal with what life throws at us.
- Practicing positivity gets easier the more you practice it.
- Know what motivates you and share that with your organization.

CHAPTER 2

Resilience

In this chapter, we will deep dive into resilience and explore how vulnerability is essential in building it. I will share some stories about how I built resilience and offer suggestions on how you might increase it for yourself.

Resilience is the capacity to recover quickly from difficulties. When we are productive and making things happen, we indirectly give ourselves opportunities to build resilience. The more we build our resiliency, the easier it is for us to bounce back from challenging situations. When we are productive, we are moving, shaking, and doing things that may or may not work out for the best. Usually, when that something doesn't work out for the best, it at least allows us to learn more about and build resilience.

We all experience challenges in our lives, not just limited to our careers or the organizations we work for. The challenge might be a death, a disease, a divorce, financial stresses, raising kids, job losses, and many other things we may have to face and navigate through. Without resiliency, we would have a tough time facing any of these challenges. If we don't build our resilience, those challenges might push us to the point of physical or mental illness.

There are different types of resilience, some being mental, emotional, and physical. Mental resilience is about being adaptable and flexible. Those who are mentally resilient can adapt quickly to changes and navigate through uncertainty. Some folks are more flexible and adaptable than others and have more resilience. Being flexible and adaptable is not always my strength, but I am stretching, growing, and practicing both of those strengths, sometimes daily. This practice is helping increase my resiliency.

Emotional resiliency is when we can control our emotions in challenging times. When folks are emotionally resilient, they can deal with challenges calmly. This type of resiliency often looks like positivity because these folks know that what does not kill them only makes them stronger. They know that the storm will eventually pass and there will be brighter days ahead.

Physical resiliency is where the body can bounce back from illness or sickness. This resiliency could be having a higher immunity, which results from all the things we do that contributes to self-care, which we will explore in Chapter Nine.

I have also read about social resiliency, which is basically how groups of people can bounce back or deal with challenges together. An example of this may be how society coped with the recent pandemic.

Resilient folks often have an optimistic outlook or attitude. They believe in themselves and are in control of themselves and their emotions. They are adaptable and flexible and can solve problems better than those with low resiliency. They are emotionally aware, have a social circle of friends and colleagues that support them, are typically light-hearted, and have an easygoing attitude. One of the new phrases I repeat to myself is: "It's not good, it's not bad; it just is." I'm unsure if that is optimistic, easygoing, or just a neutral concept, but it helps level out the high and the low times and is something I enjoy exploring.

Resilience gives people the psychological strength to cope with stress and hardship. It is also the mental reservoir of strength that people can call on in times of need to carry them through without falling apart. Resilient individuals can better handle adversity and rebuild their lives after a struggle. And we all have struggles in our everyday lives.

Everyone experiences setbacks and challenges. Life happens to all of us. By building our resilience, we are much more capable of facing those struggles head-on and work our way through them more easily.

If our resilience is low, we can become overwhelmed and focus, or even dwell on, all that is wrong rather than finding a solution or a way forward. I know that I struggle with this. One little thing happens, then another, and suddenly, I'm in a downhill spiral where everything feels heavy, dark, and out of control. At this point, I often find myself ruminating over certain things, and that's when I know it's time to get grounded and will likely go out on the ocean for a paddle and a visit with my sea lion friends.

Do you know the Serenity Prayer? "God grant me the serenity to accept the things I cannot change, the courage to change the things I can, and the wisdom to know the difference." Certain things are in our control, and other things are not. Understanding and accepting what is within our control will also build our resilience. It's the same idea as living in the present, in the now.

If there is nothing we can do about a problem or situation at the time, as it is out of our control, and we accept that, then we can shift our focus elsewhere and find something to be grateful for or enjoy, specifically in the here and now. I got to practice gratitude during my recent move up to the mountain, which helped me build my resilience.

Moving On Up

At the end of February 2023, I started a new adventure in a new location by moving my tiny home up to the side of a mountain, almost right at the top. I was moving to a place that was 2205 feet above sea level. I had purposefully built a tiny home on wheels so I could have numerous adventures and be a part of different communities. On moving day, a friend and I drove to the new spot first thing in the morning. We wanted to take a load of firewood up and check the roads. It was a beautiful day. It had snowed about four inches the night before, so there was beautiful light, fluffy snow everywhere. The grader was out plowing the road (the last five miles is a grid/gravel road), and all was well. It was a nice wide road, and it was in great shape.

After we had delivered the firewood, we headed back down the mountain to my house. We had a few delays that morning and left my previous location a few hours later than planned. It was about thirty-five minutes from the old place to my new spot where I would park my tiny house. I remember leading the mover out of my old place onto the highway towards the mountain we would have to climb. Most of the way is pavement, but as I said, the last five miles is a grid road. There are nine switchbacks on the way up the mountain, all of them being on the gravel section.

I was in front of the mover towing my house, and my friend was behind him. I didn't want to be in the way of the mover, so I would go ahead, get around the switchback and then stop and wait until I could see him again. Unfortunately, with two switchbacks remaining from the top, the house didn't come around the bend. We were two miles away from my new spot, on the gravel, and the mover had lost momentum, lost traction, and started sliding backwards down the mountain with my tiny house hooked on behind him. My house ended up in the trees and the snow where it stayed for a five-and-a-half-hour nap.

When the house (and the mover) started sliding backwards, they almost ran into my friend. She was trying to back up and get out of the way, but someone was behind her, and they weren't backing up quickly enough. When the house finally stopped sliding and landed in the trees, my friend came around and up the hill to tell me. I had already started to back up down the mountain because I knew something was wrong. I remember getting out of the car, and she just looked at me with big eyes and said, "Oh, Lana." I replied, "Is it still on its wheels?" It was.

When I drove back to the house, I jokingly told the mover, "That's not where I wanted you to park my house." He was a super guy and was very traumatized by the event, rightfully so. The shining sun that had come out that morning had melted that fluffy light snow and turned it into a sheet of ice. In fact, when I got out of my car, I shut the door, and the vehicle slid five feet down the mountain before it stopped. You couldn't even stand up on this road. It was treacherous, but we didn't know until it was too late.

It took five and a half hours, four tow trucks, and two of us directing traffic to get the house out of the ditch. At one point, the tow trucks had chains stretched across the road, and no one could get through. I remember my friend checking in on me and saying, "I can't believe you're not crying." I told her, "There's no reason to cry yet. We don't even know what we're dealing with." I had my two pups with me; they were safe, I was safe, no one was hurt, and nothing was damaged except for my house. It could have been so much worse. And my house, with everything I owned in it, remained on its wheels when it could have ended up down the mountain and demolished. It's funny how sometimes we become stronger than we expect ourselves of being capable of. You can be sure this event helped me to build resilience tenfold. It's also an example of how having a positive mindset can help us gently navigate through tough situations.

Leading up to this, I had already spent twenty-six months living in my tiny home. I had many experiences that built resilience in that time, both living tiny and specifically living tiny in the winter when things can freeze up. I faced the challenges, eventually worked out all the bugs, solved the problems, all this strengthening my resilience. One additional thing I did to prepare for the move is I made sure that I had adequate time to plan the move while still being able to work and get proper sleep in the days before the move. Taking care of myself leading up to the move also added to my resilience.

And then, just having experiences where I have been able to navigate other bumps in the road (slight pun intended) had built my resilience, knowing that things will work out; we simply need to draw on our patience, courage, and resilience to help pull us through. Above all else, this experience gave me content to use in my resilience workshops and this book. As a side note, there was less than a thousand dollars-worth of damage to my house. I used both my mental and emotional resiliency to remain calm, be patient, and trust that eventually, all would work out. And it did.

A Shitty Story

Have you ever heard of a poop pyramid? You may know what I'm talking about if you have a camper trailer and have used the toilet. Here is a shitty story I want to share, showing how even small (and smelly) situations can build resilience.

I camped my whole life with my family, from when we were kids to when I was fifty. I always felt terrible for my dad, who had to empty the black tank (where the toilet flushes go). I often used public facilities, even if it was just an outhouse. If I had to use the washroom in the middle of the night, I would usually use the one in the camper as we camped where there were bears, and I didn't need to run into one on my way to the outhouse. When I used the washroom in the camper, I made sure to use only a little water when I flushed because in my head, the tank wouldn't fill up as quickly. Do any of you smell where this story is going?

I moved into my tiny home on December 14, 2020. About seven days later, leading up to Christmas, when stores and RV dealerships would close for a handful of days, I had the realization that I should have paid more attention while camping with family now that I was essentially camping (or what some refer to as glamping) full-time as a lifestyle. I had been using my toilet and using very little water, just like when I camped all those years with my family. You can imagine how surprised I was on day seven when I went to flush and, when the trap slid open, I could see toilet paper. (For non-campers, camper toilets have a flush peddle that you step on. It releases water and opens a trap door so the waste can go into the black storage tank).

I was confused—I didn't know why or even what I was looking at. After some research, I realized I had formed a poop pyramid. I hadn't used enough water, and the solid waste just started building up (and up and up) on top of what was already there. This mountain of poop can basically turn into cement if not dealt with. This flushing situation was lesson number one and the start of resilience building while living tiny. I expect some of you would appreciate it if I stopped this story at this point, but I also know others want to know if everything came out smelling like roses in the end. Here's how it went.

One solution offered by a quick Google search was to add water to see if the pyramid would "fall." Adding water did not work. A slightly more disgusting suggestion was to add boiling water, which could melt the pyramid down. When adding boiling water to this crappy pyramid, you can only imagine the repulsive smell. I tried that for about two hours. I just kept boiling water, pouring it in, boiling water, pouring it in. The entire house smelled anything but sweet. Finally, I gave up and took my boys (my two miniature dachshunds) for a walk. While out walking, I came across a stick. I casually picked up the stick, used it as a walking stick, and took it home. I felt like I was being sneaky. I certainly didn't want anyone to know I had a poop pyramid! I had just moved in. Everyone was watching the new girl with the big new tiny home. There was only one other tiny home in this resort, so we stuck out a bit compared to the camper trailers.

I took the stick in the house, into the washroom, and yes, you guessed it, poked the pyramid with the stick. You cannot imagine the feeling of relief when I felt a release, heard a tremendous sucking noise, and finally solved the issue of the poop pyramid. It was gone. I learnt what happens when you try and save on water. I will forever use plenty of water to flush the toilet. This is how you build resilience; you have an issue (this one was super shitty), find a solution (not always do you want to wade through the problem, especially if it is shitty), and learn how to avoid it in the future. Now if this were ever to happen again (it won't in my house), I would know how to deal with it and get quicker and less smelly results.

Being Vulnerable to Build Resilience

In my team-building workshops, we often have discussions about making mistakes. I have no problem making mistakes because I know I will grow and learn from them. Building resilience is similar.

> *We can look at challenges as opportunities for growth and have a more positive mindset when life happens. That way, we will be more in control of our emotions and be able to find ways to improve our situation or work through problems.*

If I have too much going on and not enough time to rest and rejuvenate, I am emotional and impatient and have little empathy and tolerance for anyone or anything. This happens when I am not practicing self-care, which we will explore later in the book.

I learned through the recent pandemic the importance of being vulnerable by being transparent and honest with your support circle: friends, colleagues, and family. I remember in the early summer of 2021, just being so tapped out. I had moved two provinces away, changed my lifestyle to live tiny, left all my friends and family, and had gone through a merger/acquisition with the company I loved working for, and now I was miserable. Not only was there nothing left that was familiar, but I was also in a toxic work environment where individual thinking was frowned upon. My health suffered, and I was put on heart and blood pressure medications. I didn't know who to trust for information regarding the pandemic, vaccinations, or the future. It felt like I had very little support and a lot on my shoulders. I needed to be able to talk to someone to see if I was the only one struggling like this.

One morning during this time, I was on the phone with a client, and I just blurted out to her about how much I was struggling with all the instability, lack of knowledge of the particulars of the pandemic, and the division the pandemic was creating between those around me. We didn't know much about the pandemic, didn't know what was coming next, and I was tired, scared, and confused. I just wanted some normalcy.

As a result of my sharing, my client informed me that she was having many of the same feelings I was having. For some reason, folks in my circle were not talking about their feelings or if and how much they were struggling. Once I knew that I wasn't alone and others were dealing with the same doubts and emotions, I made sure to have similar conversations with others I spoke to. Sometimes you need to share what you are feeling and going through. It may not resolve the issue, but most often, you will realize that you are not alone. Sometimes this looks like venting, which in situations like this, I encourage. Being vulnerable and sharing our struggles with others increases our resiliency even more.

There are many ways to build your resilience. Similar to building confidence or practicing self-care, building resilience takes time. It is a continual effort that we have to practice regularly.

You can build your resilience by strengthening your belief in yourself. We have all been faced with challenges in life, and guess what? The fact that you are here, reading this book, means you were able to overcome those challenges. Know that no matter what you face, you will get through it eventually. By working through problems and finding solutions, we build our confidence and, in turn, also build our resilience.

As previously discussed, being positive and optimistic also increases your resiliency. Finding hope when faced with challenges and focusing on the good, no matter how hard that is to find or how small it is, builds our resilience. I know it can get exhausting when you are constantly looking for good in challenging situations. At times, it pours when we only expected a little rain. It's time for another story.

Remember when I said that sometimes one thing happens, then another, then another? This was the first other thing that occurred shortly after the move.

A Bad Break

Ten days after the move, I was out shovelling the thirty-six inches of snow we got in thirty-six hours (remember, I live at an altitude of 2205 feet above sea level, so I can get as much snow as they get on the Canadian prairies where I spent the first five decades of my life). I saw my landlady trying to get her vehicle out of the ditch, which she had slid into the night before due to the icy conditions. I helped her shovel around her car, and then a gentleman and I tried pushing her out. We were successful; however, when she started moving forward, so did I. I slipped and fell and broke the back of my wrist. This was yet another excellent opportunity to face a challenge, build resilience, and have content for resiliency training sessions and this book (that's how you find the positive in a challenging situation, my friend).

I continued to move snow with one hand, an elbow, and my neck for three more hours, if you can imagine. I thought it was just a sprain, and it was icy, so I didn't even consider going down the mountain to the hospital. In fact, I didn't get it X-rayed for four days, which is when I got my first cast. Isn't it great that these incidents happened so I had firsthand examples of building resilience to share? (Note the sarcasm.)

The two stories of my move up the mountain and breaking my wrist show how much gentler it is to navigate through challenges if you adopt a positive mindset. It was not easy in those situations at first, but one of the positive spins I put on both was that I had firsthand experience and examples for my webinars and workshops, and both outcomes could have been much worse. With the house, there was very little damage—I got to sleep in my house that night, so it took a relatively short amount of time to navigate through the situation. No one got hurt, no other vehicle was damaged; there were a lot of positives and lots to be grateful for.

And if you must break a bone, a subtle fracture to your non-dominant hand is best. It would have been way worse if I broke my right hand or, God forbid, one of my legs, ankles, or feet. That would have been way more challenging to get through. And this happened when there was still snow, so I didn't miss out on much paddleboarding, which is very important to me. Lastly, I didn't have any in-person workshops scheduled where using both hands is necessary, making everything much more manageable.

I'm not always positive, but most of the time, I am. If I get tired, run down, or have too many things happening simultaneously, I have negative moments when I think the sky is falling and life is unfair. These periods usually last only a short time. Practicing positivity gets easier the more you practice it, and likely, when you go through more life experiences and see how you can get through them, it gets easier to be positive or, at the very least, less negative. It is what it is, and most of the time, the events we struggle with are not life changing. There is the "5 by 5 rule" which states if it won't matter in five years, then it isn't worth being upset for more than five minutes. These experiences gave me a two-for-one opportunity. I was able to practice positivity while building resilience. Great deal!

And now, to finish sharing with you the rest of the downpour, I then found out my insurance had drastically increased because of having no fire protection (apparently, the municipality I now live in does not provide fire protection to anyone that lives on a gravel road—I have no words for this nonsense), my pad rent increased 33% the following month, and I wasn't previously made aware of this. Then I got my first month's hydro bill, which was basically the same amount I paid for the entire previous year. (This bill was a mistake, and I didn't end up paying for it, but it was still a challenge I had to face after facing so many others.) At this point, I almost lost my marbles. It was just too much in too short of a period of time for me to process. And I had a broken bone that impacted my ability to complete normal day-to-day activities and how my entire body felt. Only those with a broken arm/wrist/hand can comprehend how difficult it is just putting on a bra or pulling up your pants, never mind washing dishes or opening a pill bottle with a cast, especially at the beginning when you are in a lot of pain. It was almost like the universe was setting me up to write this chapter with many experiences happening within a short six weeks!

One of the biggest things that helped me navigate through the house-moving incident, the broken wrist, and all the rest was my gratitude. Remember when I told you my friend asked me, "Why aren't you crying." And I replied, "I have nothing to cry about yet." There was so much that I was grateful for. I did cry just before midnight when I finally got into bed that night, but they were tears of gratitude and relief. Life is better when you can remember that things could always be worse. So much could have gone wrong that day of the move that would have been life-altering, but it didn't. And for that, I am still and forever will be grateful.

> *Positive thinking does not mean ignoring the problem to focus on positive outcomes. It means understanding that setbacks are temporary, and that you have the skills and abilities to face your challenges.*

And if you face that same challenge again, you will have the skills and abilities to work through it much easier and quicker the next time, just like the poop pyramid. This is what resiliency is all about: building that muscle.

I just want to touch quickly on that ever-so-important self-care, which we will cover in greater detail in Chapter Nine. Ensuring you are in tip-top shape (or as good as it can be for the moment) is vital to building resilience. If we are in good condition mentally, emotionally, and physically, we are much better equipped to navigate what life throws our way. Ensure you get enough sleep, move your body, and feed it well. Take your breaks and take time for yourself. All of this will help build your resiliency.

Another way to increase your resiliency is by setting goals. If you find a challenge overwhelming, take a step back and look at what must be done to take the first step. You don't have to have the whole thing mapped out to be able to start. Set some goals, take some steps, and overcome the obstacle. Setting goals will also increase your resiliency.

The next idea I want to offer is to focus on what you know and what you have already done. Sometimes our challenge or obstacle is so huge that if we were to focus on how much we must do, we might give up and walk away. But focusing on what we have already done or know from our previous experiences makes it more surmountable. We have the tools and resources to overcome most obstacles.

In my workshops, I often speak about the concept of Plan, Do, Review, and Revise. This is important to practice when we find ourselves in a difficult situation, working through an issue or problem, or dealing with a particular challenge. If we make a plan and find it isn't working, we need to review what has worked and what hasn't and then create a revised plan. If plan A doesn't work, try plan B. It might take you going through plans C, D, E, and F. Still, whenever you do finally come through the difficulty and see the other side, you will have built your resiliency again by being able to figure out the solution and moving past the issue.

And finally, it is crucial to have a support system in place. You will need friends, family, and colleagues to lean on during tough times. We must be open, honest, and transparent with these folks, build trust, and ask for help when needed. It amazes me how sometimes all it takes is one good night's sleep, and all is right in the world again, or at the very least, I know I can wade through the muddy waters and will eventually come out and clearly see again. There is that saying, "This too shall pass." Having strong resiliency does not mean that we won't have bad things happen in our lives or that everything for us is rainbows and butterflies; it just means we have the means to navigate through those experiences and situations. In the next chapter, we will look at competition and how it can help you succeed and improve the effectiveness of an organization.

Hen House Highlights

- There are many types of resiliencies, some being: mental, emotional, physical, and social.
- When we are productive and making things happen, we indirectly give ourselves opportunities to build resilience.
- If we don't develop our resiliency, challenges might push us to the point of physical or mental illness.
- Resilience gives people the psychological strength to cope with stress and hardship.
- Knowing and accepting what is within our control will build our resilience.
- Being vulnerable can also build resilience.

CHAPTER 3

Competition

C ompetition is the last idea we will explore in part one and with regards to self. Competition is interesting and can be both positive and negative. I love competition, but only if it is fair.

In May 2020, I worked with a software company out of Winnipeg, Manitoba that created software solutions for municipal governments across Canada. I used these products when I was CAO in Southwest Saskatchewan. I loved the products, the company, the team, and the culture, so when I decided to retire from municipal government, I chose to be a part of their sales team.

My colleague Braeden and I worked closely together. We had previously built a pretty tight relationship because he was my account representative when I was a client. I remember visiting with him in person at different conventions, and there were always some laughs and great discussions.

Braeden was responsible for clients in Eastern Canada, and I was responsible for clients in Western Canada. Often, we worked on the same campaign, which we developed and designed collaboratively. If we were equally successful in a particular campaign, or close to it, I loved the competition. We would banter with each other, tease each other, and create competitive goals together. We made sure to get the whole team involved so everyone could join in the fun. This healthy type of competition was motivating for me. It was a win-win for both of us and the organization.

I had so much fun working with Braeden and the team. It was essential for us to ensure our competition was fun for our colleagues as well. Competing and obtaining new clients benefitted everyone, from management to the developers, training, and sales.

Before my working there, when Braeden obtained a new client, he would get everyone's attention by ringing a doorbell he had hidden under his desk and then playing music over the loudspeakers in the office. He usually picked a song representing the region where his new client came from. This doorbell and music were a mini celebration for all.

I had a remote position in this company. Our office was in Winnipeg, and I was then living in Southwest Saskatchewan. For the readers who don't know, football is a big thing in the Canadian prairies. One of the biggest rivalries is between the Winnipeg Blue Bombers and the Saskatchewan Roughriders. I spent five decades in Saskatchewan and love the Saskatchewan Roughriders!

My colleagues, based in Winnipeg, Manitoba, love their Winnipeg Blue Bombers equally.

It has always been a fun and friendly rivalry, so when I obtained my first client, I got one of my colleagues in Winnipeg to tap into the loudspeakers and play the Saskatchewan Roughrider theme song. She had me on a video call on her cell phone and took me through the office while the Rider's theme song was playing so I could see the reaction of the others as they heard, "Green is the colour, football is the game, we're all together and winning is our aim..." It was hilarious and way too much fun. The look of disgust of a few of my colleagues having to listen to our theme song was priceless and is one of the highlights of the time I spent with the organization. This is an excellent example of healthy competition. Shortly after that, we started using Microsoft Teams, and so when we obtained a new client, we would send a message through Microsoft Teams to the entire staff and team, with a link to a YouTube video of a great song we chose to celebrate obtaining our new client. The best days were when we played a song or two each!

If we weren't equally successful, it was no fun, and there was no benefit to the competition. We had too much respect for each other and always wanted what was best for the team. In these cases, there was less focus on the individual. When one of us was lagging or struggling, the other would find ways to encourage and support their colleague. This relationship, including the competition, worked well. We are still excellent friends, even though we both went in separate directions a few years before I started writing this book. We built our relationship and bond through this competition and helped each other when things got tough. We both were authentically happy for each other when a new client joined us, no matter whose side of the country they were from.

This position was my dream job, and I am so grateful for my time on this team. They say all good things come to an end, and unfortunately, it was true in this case as well. The business went through a merger that didn't work out well for those of us moving over in the acquired company. I learned a lot in the few years I was part of this organization, and I wouldn't trade it for the world. It was a stepping stone to what I'm doing now: consulting, training, creating, and writing. It allowed me to have some fun and still work with many of my colleagues from the municipal world by offering them software products that made their jobs much more manageable.

I started a new tradition in 2022 and flew to Winnipeg to visit my old colleagues from that organization. When planning the trip, we made sure it was when the Saskatchewan Roughriders were in town to play the Winnipeg Blue Bombers; that way, we could still be in competition and have some fun. In 2023, we went to the Banjo Bowl, which is the second most incredible Rider game to go to. (The first is the Labor Day Classic in Regina, Saskatchewan the weekend before.) The exciting yet friendly rivalry continues today.

Competition With Self

When I was CAO for local government, I tried many different forms of employee reviews and performance appraisals. One of the things I did with my staff was to help and encourage them to set goals. I taught them how to set SMART goals (Specific, Measurable, Attainable, Realistic and Timebound). I still like the idea of SMART goals, even though it is an older concept. When employees set goals at work, most of the time, they are competing with themselves. Competition with self is another essential form of competition that can help both you and the organization grow and prosper.

There are many ways that an environment with healthy competition can benefit the organization. It is a sure way to develop new ideas that drive innovation. Acknowledging that organizations compete with their rivals, I want to focus solely on competition between colleagues in the same team within the same organization at this point. In a competitive environment, folks must look for and create new ways to do things better and, for that matter, to be better themselves. They need to develop and innovate in a competitive environment, which results in the organization excelling and growing.

Not only does the organization excel, but the employee excels when they understand that their performance is being considered in comparison to others. This competition creates a sense of urgency and accountability. It pushes employees to be more creative, think outside the box, and find new procedures and ideas to meet or exceed goals and expectations. When employees do the above, they develop new skills, acquire new knowledge, and improve their performance. This growth is a win-win as when the employees push themselves, their organization also reaps the benefits of them doing so.

Healthy competition also fosters excellence. I cannot encourage perfection, which is impossible and unnecessary, but doing our best is always good. In my workshops, I express that we should be happy and accept that we are imperfectly perfect. When individuals or teams compete against one another, they attempt to use their strengths to improve their skills and abilities. They try to surpass their past achievements. This pursuit of excellence benefits the individuals involved and the organization as a whole. It also creates a culture of high performance, where employees support and push each other to reach new heights and deliver better results.

Healthy competition can even increase our self-confidence because of the impact of experiencing other folks' skills and strengths. When working with others in a trusting environment where everyone is working for the benefit of the team and the organization, we can look at what others are adding to the team. We see different perspectives, new skills, and processes that may be better than the ones we use.

I remember working with a sales team where we were creating an email campaign to offer our other products to our existing customers. We were to each come up with something that would engage our audience. One of my colleagues had thought of sending a short email asking a question and giving three or four possible answers. By seeking information that took folks almost no time to reply to, our reply percentage increased. For example, the question might be: Are you interested in learning more about our products? A) Yes, B) Yes, but at a later date, C) Not at the moment, but I will reach out to you when I am. This idea was simple for the recipient as they just had to hit reply, pick A, B, or C, and hit send. This idea may not have been his originally, as I have recently received the same type of marketing email, but at the time, it was an idea he shared with the rest of us to try in hopes of improving the results of our campaign.

Healthy competition also assists in building resilience, which I covered in the last chapter. By being competitive, we adapt to different processes when needed. We realize there are other ways of doing things, which is helpful when some of our standard procedures aren't available. This environment builds a culture of continuous learning and adaptability, which is one way to ensure long-term success for the organization.

How to Encourage Healthy Competition

Healthy competition is present primarily in healthy organizations. To give you more clarity, it takes special people and time to build an environment with inclusion and psychological safety where everyone feels secure and confident in their positions. There needs to be trust, and trust is built over time when we are willing to be vulnerable. All those factors must be in place before healthy competition can be a part of the game. And speaking of games, games are usually a lot of fun for most of us. I worked with a leader once that often said, "Everyone wants to be a part of something fun." The organization I spoke highly of in the last section had fun, and they added to it when they hired me because I am the Queen of Fun! Here is a bit more about that organization.

Folks who visited that Winnipeg office still talk about how much fun the employees must have had. There were comfy couches, a shuffleboard table, a great lunchroom/lounge, big-screen TVs, and an environment that was not only inviting but also encouraged collaboration and teamwork. I didn't witness the daily interactions because I worked remotely. Still, I was told that the organization's founder could be found almost daily playing shuffleboard with one of the employees. They had potluck lunches, went to hockey games, and celebrated anything anytime they could. It was also a diverse group of folks from many different cultures with unique personalities and backgrounds. It was heartbreaking when the company was sold, but that's business in the real world.

> *To have healthy competition in your organizations or within your teams, create an environment where it is an equal playing field, and where everyone has access to the same tools, resources, and support.*

Organizations need to determine the strengths of the individuals on their teams and then lean into those strengths. It is also beneficial to identify individual weaknesses and help folks turn those weaknesses into strengths. Share with your team what healthy competition looks like, show them you support and encourage it. Healthy competition where everyone is engaged can bring about new ideas and systems from which the entire organization can prosper.

In addition, the organization needs to put some skin in the game to encourage healthy competition. Reward those who compete and go one step above and beyond. It doesn't necessarily need to be a financial reward. The reward could be a nice lunch out with the boss. Or perhaps folks could have the opportunity to work with someone new and show them the ropes, have special responsibilities, or have input into the organization's direction. Maybe the reward is time out of the office or a day off. Whatever motivates your employees are the things you need to offer to them as a reward.

Once you understand what your team members see as a reward, you can reward them accordingly. Let the winners pick from a list, such as:

- A paid lunch with the boss;
- A special spa treatment;
- Two tickets to an event;
- A day off work;
- Sitting in on a planning meeting and having your voice heard (this is something that should occur anyway but often doesn't);
- An opportunity to spearhead an idea or event; or
- An opportunity to participate in a blue-sky session to set organizational goals for the following year.

Whatever it is, if you reward those who go the extra mile, it will often motivate others to do more. If everyone gets treated and rewarded the same, without having to do anything extra, many employees will not strive to be creative, try something new, or do anything more than necessary. Be clear on what it will take to be rewarded. Having everyone involved in developing the reward system might be a great exercise. Of course, those top performers could also receive financial compensation through wage increases, but it isn't the only way to encourage them to do more. It is a great idea to have a discussion with new hires to determine what is important to them and how they like to be rewarded.

If an organization can find a way to promote competition and show their employees that competition can be healthy and fun, then a culture for competition will be created where all are engaged. The culture also must be one of trust and compassion so that one can win gracefully and lose with honour. Because we spend a lot of time at work, it would be great to have some fun while there. Next, we will move on to part two, focusing on self in relation to others (or teams) and explore the importance of team building.

Hen House Highlights
- Competition is a sure way to develop new ideas that drive innovation.
- Healthy competition is present mainly in healthy organizations.
- Healthy competition also assists in building resilience.
- Healthy competition where everyone is engaged can bring about new ideas and systems from which the entire organization can prosper.

PART TWO

CHAPTER 4
Team Building

The true message in Heffernan's TED Talk is building solid teams with a positive mindset, high resilience, and that collaboration is more important than the individual strengths of each team member. She said, "What matters is the mortar, not just the bricks." It's really about what happens between people. She also said, "Companies don't have ideas; only people do." For these reasons, team building is critical.

In my team-building workshops, I discuss the importance of building better relationships and getting to know our colleagues better.

> *When we understand what motivates members of our team, their strengths and weaknesses, how they deal with conflict, and how to best communicate with them, we can build better relationships and stronger teams.*

Once we have this information, we can take a step back and consider some of the previous assumptions we may have made about them, often seeing that we had misconceptions. This practice helps cultivate empathy by promoting understanding and reducing making assumptions that may be incorrect.

In the Super Chickens video, Heffernan shared information regarding a study that showed successful teams had three things:

1. High empathy,
2. Inclusion (giving everyone equal opportunities to contribute), and
3. Diversity.

In her TED Talk, she said teams with more women were more successful, but it might be because they provided a diverse perspective and were possibly more empathetic. I play her YouTube video in my Super Chickens webinars, and I always enjoy watching folks' faces when they hear her say that. Obviously, it's not only women that are diverse and empathetic. Let's explore empathy, inclusion, and diversity more, beginning with empathy.

Empathy In Successful Teams

One way to describe empathy is the ability to understand and share the feelings of another. One must have a relationship with their colleagues, or anyone for that matter, to empathize with them. Relationships are built over time. To have a relationship, one must have a past, a present, and a future. If there is no past, there is no relationship. If there is no present, again, there is no relationship. And if the relationship ends, then obviously, there is no future for that relationship. These three facts are all part of relationship intelligence which I cover in Chapter Eight.

When we have empathy for others, it gives us the ability to better understand them because we have built a connection, trust, and—hopefully—a relationship with them. Empathy allows us to put ourselves in someone else's shoes, understanding their emotions and actions better, and in turn, we can respond with more compassion, support, and understanding. Empathy helps us communicate better and actively listen (listening to understand rather than to simply reply) to be able to understand different perspectives and respond in a considerate manner. It promotes open and honest dialogue, reducing misunderstandings and conflicts within the team.

Team members are more likely to cooperate, share ideas, and work towards common goals when they can empathize with others. Again, when we have built relationships with the folks on our team, we can value and respect each other's contributions, leading to a more collaborative and productive team environment.

Empathy and vulnerability go together when building trust in our teams, trust being a necessary component in all successful teams. When individuals feel seen, heard, and understood, they are more likely to trust their teammates, share their thoughts and concerns, and take risks without fear of judgment or punishment. This is all part of psychological safety. When individuals feel like they belong, they experience higher job satisfaction, increased motivation, and a sense of belonging, leading to higher retention rates and overall team happiness.

When there is opposition or conflict, empathy helps us to navigate through issues constructively. When team members empathize with each other's perspectives, they are better equipped to find mutually beneficial solutions rather than resorting to win-lose scenarios. A win-win scenario is a much better outcome. I will provide more on opposition and conflict later in this chapter.

In summary, empathy is a powerful team-building tool that strengthens communication, collaboration, trust, conflict resolution, and employee well-being. Leaders can create a positive and cohesive work environment that promotes growth, productivity, and success by cultivating empathy within a team.

How to Increase Empathy
To increase empathy, one has to build trust and to build trust, one must be willing to be vulnerable. I have said that before, but it's worth repeating because building trust is the cornerstone of a strong and healthy relationship. Creating a safe space in your organization where team members can share and explore different aspects of their positions, thoughts, and experiences is vital. There should be zero tolerance for criticizing, mocking, shaming, or any other

destructive behaviours on your teams. We will explore how to increase inclusion and promote psychological safety in Chapters Six and Seven.

There are many ways that organizations can increase empathy, starting with encouraging a culture that values understanding, compassion, and open communication. Organizations that encourage employees to truly listen to one another without judgement or interrupting will create an empathetic environment. Active listening involves giving undivided attention, seeking clarification, and validating others' perspectives.

Creating an inclusive environment that embraces diversity in all forms, including race, gender, ethnicity, age, and background, also builds empathy. Diversity brings unique perspectives and experiences, enhancing compassion and understanding. We will explore that further in one of the following sections. Encouraging employees to put themselves in others' shoes and consider different viewpoints also increases empathy.

Organizations can further build empathy by offering workshops or training sessions to develop emotional intelligence and empathy skills among employees. These workshops provide a safe space to be transparent, open, and honest and share information about oneself. When we know personal aspects about the folks we work with, it is much easier to empathize and be compassionate with them.

In their book, *The Leadership Challenge*, Kouzes and Posner (2017) state that leaders must model the way. Organizational leaders must model empathetic behaviour by actively listening, understanding, and caring for employees. When leaders prioritize empathy, it sets a positive tone for the entire organization and shows the employees what is expected of them.

Fostering teamwork and collaboration by encouraging employees to work together and learn from one another adds to the culture of empathy. Collaboration cultivates empathy by promoting shared goals, mutual support, and understanding others' strengths and challenges. The more we work with others, the more we get to know them. When we have a history with our colleagues, we are more empathetic towards them because we have gotten to know them and realized there is much more to them than just their position in the organizations. We might know about their family, their interests, their backgrounds, all which strengthen not only the empathy we have for them but also the connection and the relationship.

Inclusion and Diversity

I have so much to share on inclusion that I include an entire chapter in this book but let's quickly look at it here. In terms of leadership, and life for that matter, inclusion is what resonates with me the most. Everyone has so much to offer. They have plenty to add to conversations, ideas, and solutions. No matter their experience level, age, race, or education, they have something to add. A young adult, even a child, can look at a problem differently, in an almost innocent way. They see things in their own way. They haven't had enough time to form biases. Sometimes we are so wrapped up in proving to everyone that we know something in order to be included that sometimes we forget to be curious and look for the things we don't know. In these situations, a child or someone with less experience can offer something that many of us might not have even considered.

We all know way more than we realize. And when we recognize that, we also learn how much we don't know. Aristotle said, "The more you know, the more you know you don't know." This is such a relevant statement. In the chapter on community, I will provide suggestions on how to increase inclusion in the organization. But for now, we can move on to diversity and its effect on team building and success.

Diversity and inclusion go hand in hand. As leaders, we should include everyone because everyone has a diverse perspective to offer. That's why having everyone sitting around the table is critical. We all have had our individual experiences. No two people can live the same life. We all make different decisions for various reasons that take us in different directions and on alternate paths. Because we are all going in different directions, we have distinct stories to tell. These differences are essential. Think of how much we can learn if we listen to what others have experienced and know. To increase diversity, we must take stock of who we have on our teams and determine who is missing. Then we can attempt to fill those gaps.

Team Building When There Is Conflict
Relationships are tricky. There are many stages in a relationship, from the brand-new honeymoon stage where you get to know each other, where only the good things are visible or present, and everyone is on their best behaviour. Then after spending some time getting to know one another, some of the sticky stuff starts seeping in. The struggles,

the weaknesses, and the issues not yet dealt with (often referred to as our baggage) start appearing in this stage. This stage is where we have the opportunity to build trust. Trust is built when one is open, honest, and vulnerable and shares their ideas, experiences, and imperfections with others. Again, trust is essential in healthy relationships at work and in our personal lives.

All relationships have conflict. The relationship can fall apart if conflict isn't handled correctly, with empathy, patience, and understanding. Conflict is such a fascinating concept, and it can be healthy for organizations, similar to the healthy competition we discussed in the last chapter. When speaking of conflict, we must also talk about opposition. A lot of what I will now share I learned during my certification as a Core Strengths facilitator.

There is a difference between opposition and conflict. Opposition is good. It means there are different ideas, which is a brilliant way of finding better solutions. Opposition can also be a source of productive collaboration. If an organization can support opposition, many ideas or opinions can be shared, resulting in better outcomes. Sometimes opposition will be avoided for fear that it turns into conflict. Opposition turns into conflict if things get personal. You have entered into the conflict zone when you start accusing or pointing fingers at others. Surprisingly, conflict can be a positive thing. When we enter into conflict with someone, work through it, and resolve an issue, often, our relationship or connection has been strengthened because of it.

In my workshops, we constantly explore how we can avoid conflict. We always start with opposition. The key to staying in opposition and not going into conflict is to remain curious. If one can stay curious and keep an open mind, conflict cannot occur because we keep asking questions to help us understand the other side and don't stop asking questions until we have complete comprehension. Staying curious is a great way to explore and discover so many things. This can be as simple as asking whomever you are in opposition with to tell you more about what they are feeling or experiencing.

Another way to stay out of conflict is to be self-aware enough to know what triggers you into conflict and then to figure out and keep in mind what triggers your colleagues into conflict. This information can be established by simply having conversations and getting to know your colleagues better. Ask your colleagues what triggers them into conflict and explain how they will know you are in conflict. It's also important to know what those individuals need when they are in conflict. They may need time to process what has happened and to figure out how to move forward. They may need reassurance that, in the end, everything, including your relationship with them, will be okay. Or maybe they need you to listen to their concerns before walking away. It's only possible to know these things by first having a conversation. Knowing this about the folks you work with is important because we are all very different humans.

Team Building and Diversity

One of the biggest realizations of my life was when I realized the Creator (or the universe, or God, or whatever you identify that as) did not create us all the same. I don't mean things like skin colour, religion, or sex. I mean our thought processes and why we do what we do and say what we say.

How we approach things can differ significantly from what we see others do.

In my master's program, we did a personality assessment to help us understand ourselves and others. It was fascinating to learn the difference between introverts' and extroverts' actions. As an extrovert, I process out loud. I'm not good at processing quietly on my own. I need to talk to people about it. I need to hear it.

In comparison, an introvert typically wants to process internally and alone. Introverts like to think about whatever it is and come up with ideas or solutions before discussing it. To them, I might look like a know-it-all who doesn't know much because I think aloud to make sense of things. I expect introverts often have a stronger focus on process, whereas I, as an extrovert, have more of a focus on performance. I don't want to waste time sitting on ideas; I'd rather quickly figure something out, act on it, and move on to the next thing.

I remember once asking my council (I was their CAO) a question in a council meeting. Out of the seven elected officials, I might have received two answers. This lack of engagement frustrated me because I couldn't understand why the others refused to participate in the discussion. It wasn't until 2017, when I completed the System Deployment Inventory assessment with Core Strengths, that I realized how different we all are. As a result of completing this assessment, we all are grouped into one of seven categories of motivational value systems.

As a brief overview, some folks are focused on and care about people, others on performance, and others on process. There are other folks whose focus on those three things is almost equal, and what matters to them depends on the situation. Then, some people are focused equally on people and performance, equally on performance and process, and equally on people and process. Once we learn what our colleagues' motivations are or what they focus on, having relationships with those colleagues and the others in our lives is much simpler—if we respect and honour what we know about them. It wasn't that my council wasn't engaged in the discussion when I asked that question. Some of them just needed time to think about and process the question or the situation before contributing.

Having diversity gives organizations so many more options. To realize these options, it is imperative that you spend time getting to know the members of your teams, specifically what their strengths and skills are. I sat on a board once with some fantastic folks with diverse backgrounds. Unfortunately, because we never took the time to get to know each other's strengths, skills, and experience, we spent an entire year spinning our wheels and generally trying to reinvent the wheel. We had folks trying to accomplish tasks they had little experience in when we had other folks on the board who could have helped them learn and complete those tasks more accurately and in a more timely manner. I see organizations so focused on making money or proving their worth in the business world that they are missing one of the most critical points, their people. If organizations spent the necessary time getting to know the folks working with them, they would be able to succeed exponentially quicker. The folks on your team are the organization's greatest assets. They have a wealth of knowledge to offer. We miss out on so much potential if we don't get to know them.

Next, we will explore the importance of productivity to your team and organization.

Hen House Highlights
- Team building is the most crucial aspect of organizational effectiveness.
- Empathy allows us to put ourselves in someone else's shoes, understanding their emotions and actions better, and in turn, we can respond with more compassion, support, and understanding.
- Empathy is the ability to understand and share the feelings of another.
- When we have built relationships with the folks on our team, we can value and respect each other's contributions, leading to a more collaborative and productive team environment.
- The Creator did not create us all the same.
- The folks on your team are the organization's greatest assets.

CHAPTER 5

Productivity

Productivity is an integral part of successful teams. It's difficult to explore productivity without including a discussion on motivation, which we touched on in Chapter One. This chapter will focus on what factors contribute to, what methods increase, and what might reduce productivity.

When diving into productivity, we need to understand that folks look at productivity differently. For highly motivated people, productivity might look like a long day of work. For others who focus on work-life balance, it might look like cutting the day short and going to the kids' after-school ball game. No matter what it looks like for you, understanding productivity and how it can be increased is imperative.

In my team-building workshops, there are four different categories that most folks fall into when we talk about productivity (and motivation, which we looked at in Chapter One). In those workshops, we spend much time exploring when individuals are most engaged at work, meaning when they are most productive. In essence, we explore what motivates them. While doing this, we find that different people are motivated by different things, making them more productive. Some are motivated by a focus on people, some by a focus on performance, some by a focus on process, and others by a focus on all three things almost equally. More of that to come later in the book.

For me, and other folks like me, I love when I have many things to accomplish. If I have fifty things to do, I will likely get forty-eight of them done; however, if I only have four or five things to do, I might only get one or two of them done. I love multi-tasking and having a ton of different things to concentrate on. I thrive on making lists, planning my days, and setting goals. I need mental stimulation along with diversity and complexity to be most productive. Some might even say that they work best in an environment of chaos, where you must think and act quickly, make a plan, and then get the job done.

Again, we are all very different when it comes to productivity. Some folks like me might be most productive when they have lots going on, and they thrive when they are moving, shaking, and getting things done. Other folks might be most productive when working for and with others, building relationships, and helping others. In this case, they thrive when collaborating with others, where everyone is included and co-creating magical and beautiful things together. Others are most productive when researching, creating, or developing plans or programs, and making sense of things. These folks thrive most when researching, gathering data, and putting all that information into something valuable for their team and their organization. They ensure everything is perfect before offering it back to their colleagues for review or use. Finally, some resonate with all the above and thrive in environments where they are helping people, creating things, and have many things happening that need to be organized and executed simultaneously.

> *If organizations can establish when their employees are most productive at work, such as in the scenarios above, then they can ensure they honour those folks by putting them in environments, positions, or on projects that resonate with their motivational values.*

The employees will be more engaged doing work they excel at, and in turn, the organization flourishes.

How To Increase Productivity

To increase productivity, first determine what motivates each team member, when they are most engaged at work, and what triggers them into a state where they are no longer productive. Once you have determined that, you can give them what they need to be most productive.

As a certified Core Strengths facilitator, I use the Core Strengths SDI 2.0 assessments so that organizations can quickly and accurately determine what motivates their team. After the assessments are complete, organizations have authentic conversations to establish what is essential to the folks they work with, their strengths, how they deal with conflict, and how to communicate with them effectively.

Determining what motivates your team can be done without the assessment. The basics are asking questions, getting to know employees better, and determining what is important to them. You must build a relationship with them. Have authentic conversations with the folks you work with and be curious to learn about them and how you can help them to be more productive. This requires the employee to have self-awareness, and many folks have not considered and verbalized this awareness before. It's not usually discussed at work unless you are part of an amazingly progressive organization that puts its employees first and wants to create a dynamic team. Being open and vulnerable and sharing what is important to you builds trust and having that trust will strengthen your relationship with the folks you work with. And yes, this works for relationships outside of work as well.

Many of the other chapters in this book provide more ideas on increasing organizational productivity. For instance, in Chapter Three, we explored competition and how healthy competition will help increase productivity. To this, one can add; inclusion, having a psychologically safe environment, motivation, and bringing out the best in others as ways to increase productivity. Many of the themes in this book are connected to and result from other themes presented in various chapters. Does that make sense? It is all interconnected. It's interesting to look at those connections while considering the relationships of folks on our team.

In their book about World Cafes, Brown and Issacs (2005) state, "It appears that our memory of how to work together in healthy, productive ways has been nearly extinguished by the creeping complexity of group work, facilitation techniques, obscure analytic processes, and our own exhaustion." Complexity is something I do not resonate with or entertain in most circumstances. Effectively working together can be as simple as getting to know folks and then honouring them for what they have to contribute.

The above quote is from seventeen years ago. Imagine how the recent pandemic contributed to how we work together, compounding even more the complexities of group work referred to above. So many things changed during the pandemic. Some restrictions kept teams from being face-to-face and in-person with others. During the pandemic, some ideas and opinions created vast divides. Many folks found themselves in survival mode where there was so much unknown, and one of the ways to survive was to take one day at a time and navigate through that period as best as possible. While writing this book, I don't know if we are post-pandemic or still in it (FYI, it is fall 2023). Who would be able to establish that with certainty? As a consultant, I find myself working with teams on how to better communicate with their colleagues and how to build stronger relationships with them. It is something many seem to have lost during that extended period and is in high demand at this time.

It's interesting in Heffernan's TED Talk that the only way the individual super chickens could succeed was by suppressing the productivity of the rest. Remember that all but three of those super chickens were pecked to death.

Relationship-building and self-awareness were not on the super chickens' minds. Their only concern was personal success, which was detrimental to their productivity, and to their life for that matter.

Many factors contribute to our productivity, our lifestyle being one of the major ones. How much sleep we get, how much sunshine and exercise we can fit into our day, and what we put into our bodies to fuel ourselves all contribute to our productivity. This is all about our self-care, which we will explore in great detail in the final chapter. But let's look at that briefly right now.

How much energy do you have if you only get four hours of sleep? Or how badly do you want to take steps to conquer your goals if it's rainy out and you haven't moved much in the last few days because you are tired and lethargic? Do you have lots of energy when you feel sluggish because you ate many unhealthy snacks on the weekend or the night before? These factors all add to our productivity. It is imperative to ensure you get those eight or nine hours of sleep or whatever your body needs, to eat healthy (of course, we all deserve some treats from time to time), and to move our bodies regularly and in different ways. I'm not a health expert, but for me these points contribute to a more productive and enjoyable life. It's more challenging to be productive if we are tired and stressed. If we slept better and moved more, we would have less stress, and the pressure wouldn't affect us the same way.

Stress can stunt productivity. When one is bogged down by stress, focusing on or even caring about being productive is hard. It might be valuable to alleviate some of that stress to be more productive. There are many ways to lower your stress. Decreasing your stress levels is usually not something that happens overnight; it's a journey. A simple Google search will give you many options to begin this reduction, such as using guided imagery, meditation, progressive muscle relaxation, or deep breathing; going for a walk, hugs, aromatherapy, or lighting a candle; a healthy diet, taking stress relief supplements, participating in leisurely activities, or positive self-talk; practicing yoga, practicing gratitude, exercising more, or evaluating priorities and setting goals; social support, going out with friends, and eliminating stressors (sometimes that includes letting go of some relationships or even changing careers or jobs). We don't need to or have time to do all these things, but trying different options to lower stress will help.

Another attribute of our productivity is based on what we know and what we don't know. Sometimes we get stuck because of a lack of experience and knowledge. This lack of understanding or expertise can slow down our productivity. For example, when you have a project containing much unknown, it is easier to be productive once you can uncover some of the unknown. We sometimes get paralyzed when we look at something where everything feels like it is coming from an completely different world or seems to be an entirely different language.

We can learn and grow by reading, taking a course, learning from someone with experience, or a bazillion other ways of gathering information and knowledge that is available to us. And for that, we also need to have a desire—a curiosity—to do and know more. That may require building relationships with people with experience or learning more about the areas where we want to grow. I love the concept of curiosity. We talked about it in the last chapter as a way of staying out of conflict. Curiosity also helps us to learn and grow. And curiosity is my main focus when coaching my clients. I think it is a concept that is very much under-utilized and needs to become a bigger part of how we look at things.

When we have a lot going on in our lives, so much that time flies by and everything is constantly spinning, it's hard to be productive. When there is no space to just be, rest, rejuvenate, or recreate, we stay on that treadmill and do what we must just to get through the day. Everything is so complex. There is too much to consider. Our world feels cluttered.

Clutter is another distraction that reduces our productivity. If there is clutter all around us, it's hard to be creative and decipher what is essential in our lives, this hindering our productivity. We stay so busy moving, cleaning, organizing, and paying for all those things that contribute to the clutter that we don't have time to dream, be productive, or figure out what it is we truly desire. Clutter causes us stress because it makes things look and feel messy. We constantly worry about organizing it or hiding it when folks come to visit, and we might even have guilt about the money we spent on things we didn't need and now no longer use. It is very liberating to do what is necessary to reduce the clutter.

One of the things I did to lessen the stress in my life was deciding to live a simplistic lifestyle, which I have touched on already and will be another topic to explore in an entirely different book; however, I will share some more of it here with you in the following story.

#livingtinytolivebig

In 2020, when I retired from municipal government, I decided to minimalize and move into a lifestyle of tiny living. I had already started the long and somewhat emotional process of decluttering and releasing those things that no longer sparked joy for me. It is an emotional process because most folks have kept stuff for years because of who gave it to them, why they gave it to them, or because of a memory attached to it.

I remember when I started the decluttering journey, coming across a striped green and blue button-up sweater I had since I was sixteen. Keep in mind; I was forty-eight when I was doing this! I hadn't worn the sweater in twenty years, but I remembered (with the help of a photo) when I wore this while my uncle and I were taking a goofy picture of each other at the same time. This uncle was someone that I was extremely close with, one of my favourite humans ever, someone we lost way too early. It was hard to put that sweater in the donation pile because it reminded me of a happy time, but it was necessary. Letting go of things someone special bought or made for us is very difficult too. I remember giving away cross-stitch pictures my mom made for me as I knew there would not be room in my tiny house for them. It took a lot of time to process that it was not only okay but essential for me to let go of those things.

I had researched tiny home builders in Western Canada, specifically in Alberta. A friend and I went to both Lethbridge and Calgary (both in Southern Alberta) to visit the factories, take a tour, and meet the owners of those factories. One of the builders had a tiny home you could rent and stay in located in Fernie, British Columbia. A different friend and I stayed in this lovely tiny home, nestled into the mountains in British Columbia, for a weekend later that fall, and explored the whole tiny living idea. We took measurements of the spaces within the home so that I could go back to my traditional house and compare what I would have to live in if I did *go tiny*. I remember measuring the veranda at the entry of my traditional house where I currently resided and realizing that was the amount of space I would be moving into! This revelation almost stopped me in my tracks, but thank goodness, I persevered (one of my top three strengths, FYI).

The design of the tiny house we were staying in was excellent. Every inch of space was used to its fullest extent. Ultimately, this is the builder I chose, mainly because I knew for sure what I would be getting. In my tiny home, I have a full-sized fridge, an apartment-sized stove, a queen size bed on the main floor (as a murphy bed), a full-sized beautifully moulded bathtub, bookshelves, a television, plants galore (I can count thirty-one as I am writing this chapter), a workspace, a washing machine, and more space than I need for what I have. One of the best things about going tiny is that it takes me about seven minutes to clean my entire house! I have reduced my stress in leaps and bounds as there is so little to worry about within my tiny house. Living tiny did create some stressful learning experiences, but it also built resilience which I playfully shared with you in Chapter Two.

I processed the idea of living tiny over the next few months and realized I should be able to do this, but you only know once you take the plunge and do it. I remember thinking of a quote I often came across: "Jump and the net will appear." I sure hoped there was a net waiting for me once I decided to move forward. Once I gave the down payment and signed the contract, I felt like there was no turning back. I was too excited to try this new style of tiny living that turning back was never an option. It was something that certainly sparked joy in me.

My favourite memories growing up were camping with my family and friends. I loved being in small spaces with only what I needed and very few extras. I loved being in nature, hearing the birds, seeing the deer and the bears, sitting by the fire, reading and enjoying life, and mostly the feeling I had when there was less around me. (Before moving on, did you know there is a bird app that you can use to identify birds not only by their visuals but also by their songs? I use this all the time now, living on a mountain with many new and magnificent birds to get to know.) Camping was where I felt my best, where I felt most alive. I slept much better and relaxed; it was always a great reset. There was less to distract me, less to take care of, less to spend money on. Camping was where I could dream about and do the things that lit my soul on fire. After losing my mom (again, too early), it was time to change and live life how I wanted by seeking out and doing the things that sparked joy for me. It took me two years to downsize enough to fit into my new tiny home. I started well before even considering moving into a tiny home, and here's how it transpired.

Tidying Up

I was taking a certificate in executive coaching at Royal Roads University in Victoria, British Columbia while working full-time as CAO in local government in Southwest Saskatchewan. I had gotten used to blocking my entire calendar, day and night, into fifteen-minute segments full of the many things I needed to get done. It was the family day weekend in February, and I needed a break. I had been going non-stop for six months. I was looking for something to binge-watch on Netflix so I could get lost in it and give my mind a break.

A friend suggested Marie Kondo's *Tidying Up*. I, of course, fought this idea because I knew it would generate work, but she talked me into watching just one episode. Forty minutes later, I was pulling all the clothes out of my closet, out of bins in the basement, out of my drawers, and off racks, and piling it all on my bed. For those who have never watched *Tidying Up*, the premise is that you only keep things in your home that spark joy in you (which I have already referred to several times), including your clothes, jackets, scarves, shoes, boots, and so on. (And that's just considering what you wear.) I filled twenty-three grocery bags with clothes and such to donate to the second-hand store that weekend. And, of course, Kondo also shows you how to store your clothes better so that you can see what you have. That was such a cool concept—many of us have so much that we forget what we have as it is at the back of the closet or under a bunch of other clothes in a drawer. How liberating that experience was! As another sidenote, it is so much nicer to get dressed in the morning when you don't have fifty options of what to wear. All you have to choose from is ten or twelve of your favourite outfits. I love it.

Once I finished downsizing the clothes, I moved into other areas of my house. I started looking for things I hadn't looked at or used in the last ten years. There were lots! I started making a pile of those things and decided to use

Facebook Marketplace to try and sell some of them. I am a numbers geek (which is better than just being a geek) and I kept track of everything I had sold. I sold 269 things and made $9,699 in total on Facebook! It blew me away how much stuff I collected and, in turn, could share with someone else who it did spark joy in.

So much has changed since making that move, and I love the results. Even as I am writing this morning, I am watching the December weather. I have a goal to get out on the ocean on my paddleboard at least once every month, even in the winter months, and take a picture to share the benefits of living tiny on Vancouver Island with my friends and family on the prairies. If we only have this one life to live, I want to try and live it large. My hashtag on my Instagram account is #livingtinytolivebig. Living tiny to live big is now my focus and one of my mantras. It's also the title of my next book.

As a result of minimizing the things around me, it amazes me how much mental space I have to be creative and to be productive. When doing the things we love, it's easy to be productive. It's when we are stuck in a job, career, or even a relationship that drags us down, where we're not appreciated or valued, that productivity is lacking or tough to generate. Living a simple or minimalistic life is not only about what is in your house but also about what is in your head, what is happening on social media and who you follow, and the relationships that you have in your life. Sometimes you have to release some of those things when they no longer serve you or spark joy for you.

When you live tiny, you also free up a lot of funds. Shopping is a whole new story as you know what you already have and how much space you do or do not have for additional things.

LANA T. BAVLE

For instance, if I buy a new piece of clothing, like a sweatshirt, I must find something to release and donate to someone. I no longer have the option of impulse buying as I don't have anywhere to put it. It's fantastic not having all the unnecessary duplicates of things, like roasters, blankets, dishes, cups, knickknacks, etc. Instead of spending money on things, I can spend money on experiences. I am willing to bet a lot of money on the fact that experiences are far more motivational to us than things. When you can get out and explore beaches, forests, and other countries, meet new people, and do new things, you may find yourself inspired to tackle new ideas, go on new adventures, and be more productive. I have never bought a slow cooker or a pair of boots that motivated me in the same way (although I do love my teal Fly London boots).

More on Productivity

It takes a lot of self-awareness to realize what motivates you and what sucks the life out of you. Again, you must have the time and mental space to explore or consider how something sits with you and how it makes you feel. Many have lost the ability to be quiet and still because of how fast-paced the world is around them. Many are going at Mach speed and trying to do everything all the time. What happens if suddenly, we end up in our final days and we didn't take the time to do the things that make life worth living? It might be helpful to pause and consider that for a moment.

There are many cool things to explore and do in our province, state, region, or country. Some of it doesn't even take money (or much of it) and can add so much richness to our lives. We can visit museums, parks, trails, and

72

forests. We can join groups and clubs and do the things we are interested in. And then there's reading. Reading doesn't have to cost much as you can always borrow a book from the library or a friend. And reading can be so exciting! When you read, you can go on adventures without leaving your house's comfort (a nice option for those living in frigid temperatures in the winter months). You can learn how to do new things, how other people have succeeded, and how to add value to this life.

In summary, productivity is an essential contributor to development and success. You can do things to increase productivity, such as determining what motivates you and each of your team members, when you and they are most engaged at work, and what triggers folks into a state where they are no longer productive. After determining that, it is easier to provide what is needed for everyone to be more productive. In the next chapter, I will switch gears and explore the very important aspect of community, including inclusion and social connectedness.

Hen House Highlights
- Productivity is something we need personally to succeed, and the organizations we work for need to focus on increasing their teams' productivity.
- Productivity goes hand-in-hand with motivation.
- Productivity can be increased by having better self-awareness and by practicing continual self-care.
- Stress can stunt productivity.
- Have authentic conversations with the folks you work with and be curious to learn more about them and how you can help them to be more productive.

CHAPTER 6

Community

There are two main concepts I want to explore in this chapter that form community. One is social connectedness and the other is inclusion. Both of these concepts are a huge part of community and essential to have in our lives, not only at work but in our personal lives as well. Teams that have a strong sense of community are the ones that are the most dynamic.

Social Connectedness

In Heffernan's Super Chicken video, she spoke of social sensitivity, which is the ability of an individual to identify, perceive, and understand the signs and contexts in social interactions, meaning to what extent you know the feelings and thoughts of others and how familiar you are with the general knowledge of social norms. Let's look more now at the concept of social connectedness.

Team building requires us to be socially connected. Social connectedness has been defined as the experience of belonging to a social relationship or network. It is essential because it is how we build relationships with others, specifically with our teams and colleagues. We need those relationships with our colleagues to support, celebrate, and help each other with the challenges we will inevitably face. In Daring Greatly, Brené Brown (2012) poses, "Connection is why we're here. We are hardwired to connect with others; it's what gives purpose and meaning to our lives, and without it, there is suffering." We all need a connection to both survive and thrive.

Many struggled during the pandemic, especially those working from home with a lack of connectedness. Thank goodness for platforms like Microsoft Teams and Zoom that still allowed us some connection. We are still realizing the effects of this isolation and are trying to figure out how to overcome the changes in how we connect and communicate with others. Part of that struggle was that the connections we had with others were taken away from us in a physical manner. We couldn't go for walks at lunch with our co-workers (because many of us were working from home), couldn't just pop our head in someone's office for a quick hello, or collaborate as easily on projects as we had done in the past.

I came across a study published in the International Journal of Environmental Research and Public Health (2021). The study found that social connectedness, resilience, accountability, and trust were essential for effective mental health interventions. Mental health is and should be a concern for all organizations, now more than ever.

I'm not going to pretend to know much about this or have facts and figures, but the pandemic did a number on our mental health that we don't fully understand and still impacts many.

The pandemic was a massive disrupter in our lives. There was so much involved. There was fear, lack of knowledge, and divisions between people (including family members, friends, and colleagues) due to different beliefs and practices. I remember in the early days of the pandemic, there were people on both sides of the fence and some on the fence itself, not knowing what to think or do, specifically about masking, socializing, and vaccinating. It only took a few months for those people on either side of the fence to consider their choices the only acceptable ones. Those still sitting on the fence were almost made to make a choice, and whatever choice that was, many on the other side of the fence criticized and judged those people and their choices if they weren't the same as theirs. In some cases, those relationships were even severed.

I found it challenging because I believe in following the rules, as long as they make sense. And I will ask as many questions as I need to until I understand enough that I feel confident in making an informed decision. Deciding on how to move forward took me a long time because there were so many conflicting ideas. Organizations and leaders were willing to admit they were doing the best they could with the information they had, not knowing many things for sure. I had folks in my life that didn't respect or like that I was asking a lot of questions. They felt I should have been able to reach a conclusion much sooner. It certainly brought to light the concept of group think and how individual thinkers seemed almost to be a threat.

During the pandemic, we were all made to isolate and socially distance ourselves from others. There were no hugs or handshakes, and it really rocked our world as we knew it. We were then almost forced, no matter what our thoughts were, to get vaccinated, which some felt went against their personal or human rights. And by being forced, I am referring to the fact that at one time you were not allowed to fly, visit someone in the hospital, or attend certain public places unless you had proof of vaccination.

Being isolated was, I want to say, hard, but maybe a more accurate word is just different. I remember conversations around isolation being hard, but, in my mind, cancer is hard. Losing a job is hard. Losing a loved one is hard. Fighting in a war is hard. Isolation was not hard. It was just so different than what we had always done.

Being isolated was different from anything our generation has known. Some of us were comfortable taking a break from people, hiding in our homes, and protecting ourselves from the unknown. I used the time to do a lot of soul-searching, and I am sure many others did also. It was an opportunity for many of us to gauge whether we were on the track we wanted to be on, in our careers and our relationships, and some decided they wanted to make significant changes. One of those big changes is what has been coined as the "great resignation." Some people decided that life was too short to do things that didn't spark joy in them. Yes, that's my language now; what sparks or brings joy to our lives is my complete focus. (For more on the concept of sparking joy, search Marie Condo online, read her book or watch her Netflix Series.)

In any event, the pandemic took away our opportunity, or at least limited it, to socialize and enjoy social connectedness. It helped us realize that we still had relationships that were only out of obligation. I know I did an inventory of the relationships I had. And I did release some of those relationships because they were exhausting and no longer served me or sparked joy. They were complicated, which goes against that core values of simplicity. I don't mean to sound cold, but sometimes we have relationships that run their course. When that happens, it's okay to release them and move on to new and more productive relationships.

In life, people change and grow, albeit all at different paces and in different directions. When we grow, sometimes we drift apart from those we used to have close relationships with. This is due to having other interests or growing in different directions and realizing the relationship has given us all it can. It is expected that some relationships no longer serve us and therefore come to an end. Or that is how it was for me. It could be an age thing too. Once we reach those mid-life years, we start seeing that quality more than quantity matters in our relationships. There are folks that realize that when they are much younger, but that was not the case for me.

I believe that our success in life is directly related to the relationships we build. That doesn't mean we only build and need relationships for personal benefit; we also need them for professional reasons. Some relationships will help move your career or business forward. Others will help you grow and learn. And some simply bring you joy. Who doesn't love sitting around a fire with a friend or loved one and laughing so hard that tears run down your face? We all need relationships to be able to thrive. We also need to be quiet and still to do the same, but for now, we are focusing on social connectedness.

> *Our success in life is directly related to the relationships we build.*

We all want to find a community to belong to, a team to be part of. It is such a balance to achieve, having enough relationships and social connectedness and on the other side having adequate time to rest and just be. I expect that is the same for most of us. Many people are uncomfortable being in their own skin; they hate or avoid being alone at all costs. They may have had a more challenging time during the isolation periods than others. I think we all had a lot of feelings about isolation. We had emotions like fear, loneliness, anger, comfort (if we were alone, maybe we had less chance of getting sick), and bewilderment (what is this all about, and what can we learn from it?).

While developing my Super Chickens presentation, I found some interesting information that I want to share. Krystal Jagoo (2022) included in her article that Leela R. Magavi, MD (a Johns Hopkins-trained psychiatrist and regional medical director for Mindpath Health), said "elements inclusive of social connectedness, resilience, accountability, trust, and power-sharing may positively impact mental health interventions for individuals with chronic medical conditions."

Social connectedness can help release neurotransmitters, which is why Dr. Magavi highlights it can improve sleep, concentration, and mood. "This could consequently improve individuals' self-compassion and decrease the likelihood of engaging in unhealthy behaviours," she says. This is important stuff.

Developing relationships and having social connectedness pays off over time. When we connect with our colleagues, we are more likely to share information, ask for help, and grow simply because of that connection. It can be very lonely when we don't have those connections. When something great happens, it's fantastic to have someone to share it with. When we are struggling, having a shoulder to lean on or an ear that will listen is comforting. And by sharing tools and tricks that we have with others, it helps them to grow in new ways.

A straightforward example is technology. I am not as tech-savvy as I would like to be. I was on a Zoom call with a mentor, Kyle, discussing an upcoming workshop on team building that I was developing. He suggested that I project my smartphone screen onto my laptop and, in turn, onto the projector (and on to the screen) to demo an excellent smartphone app I wanted to share with my audience. I laughed and said I had no clue how to do that; it was too complicated. He took a few minutes to walk me through the simple steps, and I learnt how to project my smartphone screen onto a different device. I have likely used that learning more than fifty times in the last year, and I learnt it from the relationship and connection I had built with Kyle.

We have many opportunities to grow, stretch, and learn from our connections. Everyone is an expert at something, and I understand much better when I can see how something works. If someone can show me just once, I can grasp the concept, make notes on the process, and then practice until I completely understand and have nailed it down. When we are given the opportunity to learn from our connections, we develop new skills, increase our self-worth, strengthen our confidence, and likely find a new respect for that person as they just helped us to learn and grow. I would even say that these connections can promote better physical health. I remember having office competitions in one organization around health goals, sometimes it was a step challenge, workout challenge, yoga challenge, or a weight loss challenge. When those connections are present, we are more likely to participate in these activities, whereas if there were no connections, we might only sit back and watch, having no real desire to join in.

When I started my consulting practice full-time, facilitating workshops on leadership development and team building, mentoring, and coaching, most of my initial clients were folks I had connections with in the past and many I had previously worked with in different organizations. I had built those relationships and strengthened the bonds so well that when I started my new business, many colleagues reached out and supported me in my new venture. It proves that if we intentionally build connections and relationships, they can last a very long time and pop up after years in ways that again support us and help us grow and prosper.

How to Improve Social Connectedness

One way your organization can improve its social connectedness is to create a social committee that offers ways to interact with colleagues. The organization also needs to create space and time for these connections. A social committee can be created virtually, which is important because many organizations have adopted a hybrid work model. In a previous organization I worked for, I was a leader on a social committee, and we planned lots of fun things. We had a thirty-day yoga challenge, a recipe contest for holiday treats in December, and self-care Bingo where you had to get three lines from many activities that promoted self-care. Lots of folks participated in these activities. My favourite was an online crib tournament. Many of us would call our opponents through Microsoft Teams and play while visiting virtually. What an excellent opportunity to get to know each other and strengthen those connection by doing something fun.

Plan events and get-togethers to create a social culture. An organization I used to work for would have lunchtime potlucks throughout the year. The organization focused on hiring diverse individuals, so imagine how delicious those lunches were! Someone must be focused on people and bringing them together in your organization. If you don't have that person, I suggest you find them.

Theodore Roosevelt shared that the most important single ingredient in the formula of success is knowing how to get along with people. I have been focused on building relationships for decades. And I build relationships with young and old, well-off and struggling, highly educated and those starting on their journeys, with absolutely anyone and everyone. I am the type who always reaches out, checks in, and plans get-togethers and events. I care about people and enjoy building relationships from which we can grow and learn. And we can learn from everyone. Everyone has something valuable to contribute to our relationships and to life.

Without social connectedness, it would be a very lonely world. Not having those connections severely limits our success and our happiness. With social connectedness comes inclusion. That's what we will look at next.

Inclusion

We briefly touched on inclusion in Chapter Four. Now we can take a deeper dive into the topic. I will discuss what inclusion looks like, the importance of leading with love, and how to create an inclusive environment.

In Heffernan's video, she says that what happens between people is what really counts. She states that ideas can flow and grow in groups that are highly attuned and sensitive to each other. Isn't this what all organizations want? This idea refers to inclusion, which we will explore here, and to psychological safety, which is the next chapter's topic in Part Three.

The important thing to talk about here is how the individual members of a team become highly attuned to their teammates, as previously mentioned. In my team-building workshops, my participants complete a thirty-minute personality assessment through Core Strengths to learn what motivates them and how others are often motivated. We refer to that as someone's motivational value system or their MVS. When we understand why people do what they do, why they say what they say and what is important to them, we can improve how we work with them, helping the whole team succeed.

In 2020, I completed a master's degree in leadership at Royal Roads University (RRU) in Victoria, British Columbia. Before I started the program, I thought I knew what leadership was, but I soon learned it was so much more. I knew leaders had followers; in reality, that's all I knew. In the program, one of the first things we studied was the different styles of leadership and the ones that resonated with me mostly were inclusive leadership, shared leadership, and co-leadership, which are all very similar.

I love everything about leadership and, equally, everything about inclusion. We have so much to learn about both. I am a numbers person, not a history buff, but I believe we live in one of the most significant times when we desperately need leadership in every corner of our lives. We are dealing with so many threats, from racism to wars, to corruption, to climate change. The list is long, and we need strong leadership to help us navigate these concerns.

Diana Whitney (2010) said, "People want leadership that is inclusive, that invites the ideas, thoughts, and feelings of diverse people; and that recognizes and affirms the good work of many different people." In that same book, she writes, "In order for decisions and plans for the future to satisfy and serve diverse groups of people, all the people whose future it is must be invited into a relationship and included in the dialogue and decision making."

I developed a workshop on inclusivity in the workplace a few years ago. In that workshop, I explained that inclusion is about making individuals feel welcome and valued because of their differences, not tolerated despite them. When people feel included, they commit to the project, the team, and the organization. When they're committed, they'll make more effort, voice more ideas, and innovate more. They end the workday feeling energized, not drained, and discouraged.

The leader who says, "This is what I think is the solution," makes space for one brain in the room: their own. The leader who says, "This is the issue; what are your solutions?" makes space for as many brains in the room as there are people. They multiply the IQ of the group rather than diluting it. Including everyone is brilliant and is what inclusive leadership is all about.

It's crucial for leaders to know what they don't know and to lean on the people around them to come up with better solutions collectively. Every team member is an expert on something and can be a leader somehow. The challenge is to create an inclusive environment where everyone feels comfortable speaking up. When they speak up, and you can get to know them better, you will be able to see what their strengths and experiences are, and then when those are needed in a specific situation, you will know who you can call on.

Leading With Love

I remember a conversation at an in-person session at RRU in 2019. The program was blended learning, so we did most of our work online but did go to campus for two two-week sessions. The second time I was on campus, I packed up early in the morning and waited outside for my taxi to take me to the airport. One of the security guards was outside and was chatting with me. He asked me what I had learned during this time on campus. I replied, "I have learnt that the world needs us to lead with love," and I still believe that. It's not about power or prestige. We need love, acceptance, and understanding more than anything right now. I don't know how to convince all leaders to act this way, but I do know I can do it myself by modelling the way and leading with love. I am surrounded by many lovely humans who also believe and practice this. And many folks around the world lead in this way. Hopefully, it's like a domino effect, and if people witness others leading with love and the benefits of doing so, they will try to lead the same way.

How to Create an Inclusive Environment

We must also explore diversity and equity when discussing creating an inclusive environment. Organizations first need to have an approach that puts these three things at the forefront of everything they do. They must walk the walk, talk the talk, and model the way.

For larger organizations, this must start at the top. The organization needs to have the buy-in from the leadership team, who commit daily to diversity, equity, and inclusion (DEI) in every interaction. Only then will this approach be passed down throughout the entire organization.

I want to reference again a process I often use: the model of Plan, Do, Review, and Revise. This process is necessary when creating an inclusive environment and culture. The organization needs to determine where they currently sit with DEI. Someone may have to come in to analyze and identify what is already there for inclusion and note any significant gaps. Only after that happens can the organization make the necessary additions to the team.

In the research for my thesis, I learnt that collecting this type of data could include using surveys, focus groups, one-on-one interviews, a world café, or one of many other methods. Once the organization determines what they have and what is missing, it can then take steps to balance that out and fill in the gaps. This process might include adding different groups of folks in new hires, training in the importance of DEI, putting policies into place, etc. Once that happens, there can be a review to see where things lie. If need be, the organization might need to revise a plan to improve its DEI.

Once this process is established, ensuring all employees know the policies, participate in training, and understand the expectations regarding DEI are all very important. Again, this originates from the top down. First, the leadership team needs to understand the action plan thoroughly; then, they can share the information with those that report to them.

> *An organization with a culture of psychological safety will already have a culture of inclusion where folks practice active listening and are willing and able to have discussions that will expand the organization's greatness.*

They will also provide feedback, feeling safe when doing so. Again, we will further explore psychological safety in the following chapter.

When we discussed competition in Chapter Three, I suggested that an organization provide all employees with the same resources and tools to make things equal. Putting everyone on a similar playing field is another thing teams must do to promote DEI. Everyone must have access to training and other opportunities such as mentorships, promotions, and personal or professional development.

When creating a plan for increasing diversity, the obvious action would pertain to hiring. Once the organization has established the gaps in the diversity of its employees, it can seek to fill that gap again with the new hires. Even while the gaps are being filled, diversity can be encouraged, and engagement in diversity can result from developing opportunities for different folks to share their unique differences. Promoting diversity could include fun events like those potluck lunches I talked about, sharing different traditions at different times of the year (such as Christmas or even around birthdays), or even simply spotlighting folks from different teams at different times.

At that previous organization where I led a social committee, we introduced a ten-minute employee spotlight in our weekly team calls. These spotlight sessions were done on the Microsoft Teams platform at the time, as we had a hybrid work model where only some were in the office. We had folks volunteer each week to share information about themselves with the entire team. Some folks created a presentation, showing others where they came from, what foods they loved to eat, what they liked to do in their downtime, and maybe something about their pets (many of us have pets—more so now post-pandemic). There was always time at the end of the presentation for questions and answers. It was a great way to learn about our colleagues and their backgrounds and cultures.

Creating an inclusive environment is a journey rather than a destination. It is something the organization needs to monitor and improve continually. The cycle of planning, doing, reviewing, and revising is ongoing, as are the training and growth opportunities. The commitment must remain strong, and discussions must occur continually. I mentioned earlier that inclusion and psychological safety are closely related. Let's explore the latter now in the following chapter.

Hen House Highlights

- We all need a connection to survive and thrive.
- Social connectedness, resilience, accountability, and trust are essential for effective mental health interventions.
- We have many opportunities to grow, stretch, and learn from our connections.
- Inclusion is about making individuals feel welcome and valued because of their differences, not tolerated despite them.
- When people feel included, they commit to the project, the team, and the organization.
- It's crucial for leaders to know what they don't know and to lean on the people around them to come up with better solutions collectively.

PART THREE

CHAPTER 7

Psychological Safety

Amy Edmondson (2019), an American scholar of leadership, teaming and organizational learning and a professor of leadership at Harvard, defines psychological safety as "a shared belief held by members of a team that the team is safe for interpersonal risk-taking." She also poses that, "when people have psychological safety at work, they feel comfortable sharing concerns and mistakes without fear of embarrassment or retribution."

I once had a client who was part of an organization where neither their manager nor the organization provided psychological safety to their employees. They had a manager who did not have a lot of experience in the industry they worked in and was perhaps trying to prove himself. As a direct report, they were expected to do as they were told without asking questions or offering suggestions, even if they had more experience than the manager. They were penalized for challenging him on his ideas or not doing as told.

This manager had his favourites, and when my client played the game and drank the Kool-Aid, they were the favourite, but that only happened at the beginning, when they were eager to please. The manager, having his favourites and treating them better than the rest, broke all the rules of inclusion, providing psychological safety, building community, and team building.

The interesting thing is that this manager had a tremendous turnover rate on his team. For instance, eight out of nine folks on his team left during a period of only nine months. The organization couldn't fill the vacancies as fast as they were happening. Upper management didn't seem to notice the high turnover rate and therefore did nothing to understand or further prevent if from happening. No one was watching what was going on or keeping track of turnover. My client shared stories about the lack of psychological safety, including how one individual ended up on medication for her anxiety as a result of refusing to work nights and on weekends because of the pressures of the organization. She felt she had to plow through and get the work done without objection, or she would be punished and perhaps even terminated.

From what my client shared, this particular organization was huge and lacked leadership in every department. The culture was dark and murky. Some people liked what they were doing but finding more than a few who enjoyed working for the organization, it sounded like, would be tough. No one in a management or leadership role got it, and by it, I mean the importance of the folks that worked for them, along with the importance of psychological safety. To reiterate from a previous chapter, the employees of an organization are its biggest and most valuable asset. This organization's main focus was money, which is not the proven way to succeed. Unfortunately, we see this in organizations in every industry or sector. When you put money ahead of your people, chances of success are dismal. Although I have founded three companies in my lifetime, I don't pretend to be a business guru. These are just my thoughts that have come from my experiences, research, and the stories shared with me by my clients.

This organization didn't value its folks, nor did it take the time to build relationships with their employees, find out what motivated them, their strengths, or how they dealt with conflict. Apparently, one of the manager's supervisors had one-on-ones with some of his remaining team after the mass exodus began, but nothing was visibly done with the information she collected. It doesn't look good to those remaining when data is given, concerns are voiced, and no action is taken. The exodus apparently continued. The organization had terrible online reviews, but again, no one in management or leadership seemed to care. This was clearly not their priority.

The environment became too unhealthy, and my client finally chose to resign. She could not sleep for more than about four or five hours per night before she would wake up and ruminate over what had happened at work the previous day or what might happen tomorrow. The reality was that her health was deteriorating and fast. She had gained weight, was now having heart issues, and experienced anxiety attacks on a regular basis. She strongly felt this was entirely due to her work environment, and I tended to agree.

Almost a year after leaving that toxic environment, she had lost some weight, was sleeping better, and no longer had anxiety attacks. The results of working in an unhealthy environment full of stress can sneak up quickly. This experience with my client helped me to further realize the importance of psychological safety. Understanding how being in a toxic work environment can impact your health is a critical concept.

Employees are looking for an environment where they can thrive, not an environment where they are afraid of what will happen if they don't do as they are told, whether it makes sense or not. Edmondson (2019) states, "In the twenty-first century, high psychological safety will increasingly become a term of employment, and organizations that don't supply it will bleed out their top talent." This, along with the great resignation I spoke of earlier, will hopefully force organizations to provide the environments we all should have the opportunity to work in.

How to Promote Psychological Safety

> *"People don't leave bad jobs; they leave bad bosses or managers."*

This old axiom goes to show that providing a psychologically safe environment is one way to retain good talent.

I recently developed a workshop on Psychological Safety that offers five steps to promote psychological safety:

1. Communicate with your employees.

2. Practice active listening.
3. Model the way.
4. Stay curious.
5. Share information with your teams on psychological safety and assure them it is a priority of the organization.

Let's take a closer look at each one of those.

Communicate With Your Employees

With a master's degree in leadership, one would likely assume I have consulted mostly on issues surrounding leadership, but what I find is currently more in demand is how to build relationships and effectively communicate with folks in your organization, especially your employees. One of the most important aspects of psychological safety is getting to know your employees and, in turn, letting them get to know you. In essence, it is building a relationship with them.

I have owned businesses where I have hired staff, have had management positions, and been an employee myself. When I talk about communicating with your employees and building relationships with them, I'm not suggesting you become best friends and spend every weekend together; in fact, I highly recommend not going to that extent. I think it's necessary to have boundaries in the relationships you have at work in order to keep those relationships in check. You must communicate with your employees to understand them, what motivates and engages them, and what you can offer to help them succeed.

Remember the company I sold software products for? I knew the founder before I was an employee. I shared with you I was first their client. I knew about some of his history, how he started his business, and what kind of cool things he had done in the past. I shared with him some of the things I had accomplished, my aspirations, and some of the struggles I had experienced in past careers. The main reason I went to work for him is because of the relationship I had built with him and how much respect I had for him and the organization he had created. Every single person that worked with him was professional, knowledgeable, kind, caring, and helpful, and they all seemed to love what they were doing. When I think of it, not one person left the company while I was there. That alone shows that psychological safety was definitely a part of their culture.

It is imperative that you have conversations with your employees to uncover more about them. To begin, you might ask them the following questions:

- What does success look like for you in our organization?
- What do you want to learn more about in your position?
- What does a perfect day at work look like for you?
- Why did you decide to work for this organization?
- Where do you hope to be in five years from now in your career?

Imagine all that you might learn by asking the questions above! And those are just five simple questions. If you were to take time on a regular basis and have conversations with your folks, you would be building loyalty with them just because you are showing you are interested and that you care. This loyalty will definitely help your organization to thrive.

Practice Active Listening

I have already said this many times in this book, but it is such an important point, and many still don't practice it. Again, my degree is in leadership as opposed to psychology, so I don't understand why most folks just don't actively listen. In case you were skimming any previous sections and missed it, active listening is listening to understand, not simply to reply.

It seems that most conversations I am a part of, or even just witness, are ones where I can see the other person almost on the edge of their seat, impatiently waiting for the other to stop talking so they can interject. They keep opening their mouth and might lean forward, then close it and reluctantly lean back again. I still find myself doing the same thing at times, and I have been practicing active listening for close to a decade. I get it. Sometimes someone is speaking of something in particular that sparks a memory you want to share, and you hope they stop talking before you forget what you want to share. (Or is that just me? I doubt it.)

When you are having those conversations with your employees, getting to know them, and giving them the opportunity to get to know you, actually listen to what they are saying. When you practice active listening, you can ask clarifying questions to ensure you understand. It's very similar to taking a coach approach with someone. For example, maybe you asked them a question from the previous section, such as, "What does success look like for you in our organization?" If they answer that they want to be your top seller by the end of my first year, you might ask them a follow-up question like, "Why is that important to you?" They might share with you that they are planning a family and want to buy a larger house. That is a very basic example but look at what you have learned about that individual. They sound like a high achiever, they have goals, they want a family, and they have a plan. Now you can provide them with opportunities that will help them move towards being your top seller. You asked questions, listened to what they had to offer, and now you can better support them moving forward.

Active listening does not mean you cannot share your own stories or information. It only means that you are being intent on hearing what your employees have to say. It is totally acceptable for you to share with them some of the same information after they have finished sharing with you. In fact, that is a must in allowing them to get to know you. Of course, this has a two-fold benefit. Not only are you getting to know each other, but you are also building trust. You're asking questions, listening to understand, being vulnerable and sharing some personal information, and as I have shared in previous chapters, this resulting in building trust. Trust is also something that promotes loyalty. When you trust the folks you work with, you will typically do what is necessary to ensure everyone succeeds.

Model the Way

I first shared this term with you in Chapter Four on Team Building, specifically in terms of increasing empathy. Leaders in organizations need to model the way (walk the walk and talk the talk) when it comes promoting psychological safety. They need to show their employees that it is okay (and perhaps even encouraged) to make mistakes and share that information with others.

It's never okay to shame someone, belittle them, bully them, or make fun of them. And it's never okay to witness someone else doing those things and not intervening. Leaders, managers, supervisors, directors, and all other employees, for that matter, need to step up and put a stop to any of that unacceptable behaviour.

Organizations must share with their employees what is expected regarding psychological safety and then ensure that everyone follows those expectations, including themselves. If someone in a leadership role makes a mistake and doesn't follow this protocol, once they realize their mistake, they need to bring it to light and apologize to the team. What an excellent act in strengthening psychological safety! If this is new to the organization, know that it will take time, mistakes will be made, and there will need to be some difficult conversations. Those difficult conversations will strengthen psychological safety at the same time as building trust. There is no room for egos when promoting psychological safety so they will need to be checked at the door.

Psychological safety also includes being respectful of others and allowing them to tell their own story. If it's not your story to tell, don't tell it. When speaking about others, speak like they are in the room. Never say anything you wouldn't say in front of them and assume that whatever you say will be repeated to them. This will help you to only share necessary and positive information with others about their colleagues. If you have issues with an employee, make sure you talk *to* them, rather than *about* them.

Stay Curious

Staying curious does not only pertain to asking questions. It is also about considering how you can grow as an individual, grow the organization, and grow your knowledge. It includes providing and asking for feedback. Stay curious and find ways to improve yourself, your team, and your organization.

Have you ever heard the phrase criticize in private, praise in public? This is something that must always be practiced. If you were to criticize an employee in front of their peers, no matter how hard you have worked on promoting psychological safety, all your efforts could be lost. You will not only break the trust of that individual but of everyone witnessing the criticism. You can be sure anyone not present will hear about it. Praising in public will promote psychological safety as you will be showing your employees that you see and value their hard work, input, ideas, and contributions. Acknowledge their accomplishments and then find out how you can support them even further.

We hopefully never stop growing. Albert Einstein said when you stop learning, you start dying. Once you are able to praise someone for their contributions, ask them what is next. Ask them what support they need from you and the organization. By investing in their growth, you are investing in the organization's growth.

And finally, don't forget to ask them for feedback as well. It is imperative that you humbly accept their feedback, the very first time and every time thereafter because one sure way to stop the feedback from coming and destroying psychological safety is to get defensive when receiving feedback. Make sure you act on the feedback and thank the individual for helping you grow. This, for some, will take a bit of practice but will be a gift to both you and the organization in the end.

Make Psychological Safety a Priority

The above suggestions are all a part of this concept. To reiterate, to make psychological safety a priority, you need to communicate with your employees, get to know them and help them get to know you. You need to practice active listening and be intentional in your conversations with them. Create the space for making mistakes and admitting when you don't know something so that the employees can see it's safe for them to do so as well. And then stay curious. Ask for help to grow in the form of feedback and give them the same gift.

Sit down with your team and have a group discussion about psychological safety: what it looks like in your organization, why it is important, and how you can improve it. If you invite everyone to sit around the table to have this conversation, you will have a much easier time getting buy-in and starting off on the right foot. These conversations need to happen more than once; it's not a one-and-done. Perhaps it's quarterly, to begin with, and then semi-annually or annually after that. There are always folks willing to come into your organization and provide a refresher or specific training on psychological safety if that is required.

You can also have conversations with the entire team about who is doing things right and what needs to improve for the team to thrive even more. Ensuring the environment is respectful during these discussions will guarantee group participation where folks are excited to grow and expand. And make sure that everyone has the opportunity to contribute. Perhaps once one member offers a suggestion, they sit back and only offer other suggestions after everyone else has had a chance to participate in the conversation.

One final suggestion I want to offer here is to have check-ins and check-outs. I have done this in a few different ways. One is to simply ask each person to offer one word on how they are feeling at the beginning of the meeting and then do the same at the end of the session. Another idea that might be more fun is asking them for a weather forecast. They offer the group a weather analogy to describe how they are feeling, such as sunny, stormy, kind of cloudy, calm, etc. If this sounds corny or woo-woo to you, try it once. You might be surprised by how the group engages in this activity and it gives you an idea of where everyone is at before and after those meetings. It will feel more natural the next time you do it. Now let's learn more about the concept of relationship intelligence.

Hen House Highlights
- Psychological safety is the ability to show and employ oneself without fear of negative self-image, status, or career consequences.
- The employees of an organization are its most significant and most valuable asset.
- Providing a psychologically safe environment is one way to retain good talent.

- Promote psychological safety by communicating with your employees, practicing active listening, modeling the way, staying curious, and making psychological safety a priority.

CHAPTER 8
Relationship Intelligence

Relationship Intelligence is a concept developed by Core Strengths, of which I am a certified facilitator, as you already know. This tool is the starting block for most of my consulting services, especially in executive coaching, team building, and leadership development.

I first took a Core Strength assessment in 2017 when completing my executive coaching certificate. I have completed many other assessments, like Meyer Briggs, Disc, Colors, etc., but the Core Strengths assessment has stuck with me. I love and use it because it's comprehensible, easy to understand, and is highly accurate. A quick Google search tells us that as of 2021, over five million folks have taken the assessment. It is a great tool that provides the foundation for organizational effectiveness and has been around for a long time.

Core Strengths is a workplace assessment and training provider that has existed since 1971. Core Strengths explains relationship intelligence as four skills being; positive regard (treating people, including oneself, with dignity and respect, and assuming positive intention and motives—everyone is doing the best they can with what they have), personal accountability (taking ownership and initiative—being responsible for the results of your actions and choices), service orientation (being curious and open to learn what people need, willing to meet other people's needs, and appreciate when they meet yours) and strengths-based agility (the intentional use of behavioural strengths in pursuit of desired outcomes—metaphorically, choosing the right tool for the job).

These skills are applied in three ways. The first is by recasting the past. Once we learn more about ourselves and others, we can take a step back, ponder past events, and consider if there was more involved than we knew at the time. Often, we will find that we have some misconceptions about the meaning behind a specific event, action, or comment.

The second way we apply these skills is by co-creating the future. Knowing how our colleagues are motivated, what their strengths are, how they deal with conflict, and how to effectively communicate with them allows us to deal with them in a way that honours them.

The third is mastering the moment, which happens in our day-to-day interactions. We apply these skills to our relationships through shared experiences, present interactions, and aligned expectations to improve relationships by building trust, generating commitment, and driving results.

When I first started facilitating my team building workshops, being someone who has a focus on both performance and process, with more focus on performance, I made sure to have a solid plan for my workshop sessions. I create a detailed agenda that guides me through every minute of a six-hour workshop. For those of us more focussed on performance, we like to make a plan and stick with it. It is highly uncomfortable for us if someone throws a last-minute change our way because we feel we have to create a new plan now to succeed, and now we have less time to do it in.

I remember facilitating one of my first team-building workshops, which I did in two three-hour sessions. The team I was working with was super engaged. Many rich conversations were happening, which I hadn't planned for. During this session, I remember being constantly worried about where we were on my agenda because I felt I needed to get through all five modules or sections of my workshop, and I thought I needed to stick to a schedule to accomplish this. Even though it was uncomfortable, I held back from stopping those rich conversations because I could tell that the participants were learning, not so much from my slides and agenda, but rather from sharing their own experiences and stories and learning from each other. Again, stories are an effective way to learn, which is why I share many in this book.

When we were done with our first three-hour session, I admitted to the team that we were off the agenda, and I had to review what we had covered and revise the agenda for our next session, which was taking place the following morning. When I sat down to check what we had missed,

I realized that we had covered everything I had on the agenda; we just used the knowledge and experiences of the participants to learn rather than my slides. That was a powerful insight for me. What I learnt that day is facilitating is more than getting through some slides. It is nudging conversations in directions where the folks present can learn from each other. Since then, I have paid less attention to my detailed agenda than I do to the focus and engagement of the conversations.

Another key realization for me was that folks know so much, and sometimes we need to uncover how much knowledge they already have. For example, in a workshop, someone might ask me a question. If it is a question that will promote rich discussion, and whether I have an answer or not, I often will reply with, "That is a great question. What do you think?"

> *Almost always, when someone asks a question, they already have an answer in mind and are looking for validation that their answer is correct.*

Once the individual who asked the question gives the group their answer, I will ask if anyone has anything else to add. Sometimes these are the most incredible learning opportunities, not only for the folks in my workshop but also for myself. I love it when those learnings happen organically!

Our lives seem so busy nowadays, as we are in constant meetings, doing things with the kids and taking them places, fulfilling our family commitments, and trying to practice self-care, including getting proper exercise and sleep. Relationships and social interactions for many have become their last priority, which needs attention. Relationships are a necessity in our lives as we discussed in Chapter Six on Community.

The relationships we build are essential in both our personal and our professional life. Building relationships takes time and energy and sometimes can be tricky. And all relationships—and what we get from them—are entirely different.

There is not one person who can fulfill everything that we need in just one relationship. We get different things from different people. For example, we could go paddleboarding with one of our friends, and we might like to travel with a different friend. We may have a relationship with someone in the same position or career as us; another relationship with someone who mentors us. We have acquaintances and friends who have gone through similar situations, such as losing a parent, getting married, having a baby, or starting a new career. No one person can be all those things to us. This is why we need to have and invest in relationships with different folks.

An interesting idea to entertain is that building and maintaining relationships also helps increase our resilience (which we explored back in Chapter Two). Suppose we invest our time and energy into building relationships and getting to know people, what skills they offer, and what experiences they've been through. When we find ourselves in challenging situations or life experiences, we can then reach out to those people for support and help, a little resilience boost. It's impossible for us to know and have experienced everything. When we build relationships with diverse people, it simply expands what we have access to for that knowledge and experience.

Some other benefits to building relationships are increasing your support system, having more shared experiences, having a sense of belonging (we discussed the importance of social connectedness back in Chapter Six), having more tools in your toolbox, and having additional opportunities to have fun and hopefully live life to its fullest.

One thing that comes to mind about relationships and their importance is a quote from Jim Rohn: "You are the average of the five people you surround yourself with." If you surround yourself with people who love to cook, you'll become a better cook. If you surround yourself with leaders, you will likely learn new leadership skills and practices. If you surround yourself with people who are constantly growing and learning, you probably will find more opportunities to grow and learn. Be intentional about the relationships you nurture.

Building New Relationships

Some of the following information might seem very basic to many readers, but sometimes we need a simple reminder. Remember, I'm all about simplicity! We have already established that building relationships with our colleagues in our organizations can increase positivity, build resilience, obviously lend to team building, increase productivity, build community, and promote psychological safety. Let's look at what we can do individually to build these relationships.

Some ways that you can build new relationships would be to join different groups. For example, you could join a paddleboarding group or take part in some classes like yoga or pottery, or join a chamber of commerce or a leadership group, a mastermind group, or even a book club. If you do this, you're going to meet other people with the same interests, with the same focus in their lives as you, giving you something in common, which makes it much easier to build those relationships.

Of course, there are other ways to build new relationships. One thing you can do is participate in something you're interested in, like a marathon, a paint night, going to the gym, or taking a class. Another asset to building relationships is to be outgoing, which might be difficult for somebody who is an introvert. For those of you who are introverted, start by making small talk. Talk about the weather, your kids, a new recipe you've tried, or a book you've read. Find something relatable to the person you are interacting with and go from there. Remember, it takes time and energy to build relationships.

One of the things that I learnt in the last decade is that all you need to do to engage with someone is ask that person about themselves. Ask them how their kids are doing, how work is going, or if they are going on vacation this summer. People usually like to talk about themselves, and if you give them the opportunity to share with you what's important to them, it shows that you are interested and genuinely care. In turn, they will be happy to share that information with you, and likely they'll ask you those same kinds of questions in return.

Relationships must be a give-and-take; they can't be one-sided. If it is one-sided, it gets old fast. You must provide value to that relationship and contribute to it in order for the relationship to flourish. You have to take the time to reach out to your friends and acquaintances; you can't always wait for them to reach out to you. Take the time to plan things you can do together; again, you can't always rely on them to do this. If you're the one who is always doing all the work, making all the plans, and constantly reaching out, you might want to look for and invest in a more balanced relationship.

Another great way to build stronger relationships is to be grateful and appreciate what the other person is contributing. If we show gratitude and appreciation to other people, it makes them want to do more with and for us, and if they offer us appreciation and gratitude, we want to do more with and for them. Sometimes it's just as easy as saying thank you. I enjoy sending cool greeting cards to people. I pick up cards everywhere I go, and I love finding local artists who make cards because I share part of the culture of where I am when I send that card. I like popping a message in a card and throwing it in the mail to somebody I've just spent some time with, recently met, or just started working with. It's so much fun getting nice things in the mail besides bills and junk mail. (Do folks even get bills in the mail anymore?)

Benefits of Building Relationships

Let's consider some of the personal benefits of building relationships. I first want to explore how relationships can boost our mental health and, in turn, our mood. Being an extrovert, I know that if I find myself stressed out or overwhelmed, I need to be able to talk things out with somebody because I process verbally. Often all I need is to reach out to a friend and have a fifteen- or twenty-minute visit, which will shift my mindset and boost my mood. It's funny how in a short conversation, you can have two or three laughs, share a couple of things going on in your life, maybe a challenge you are facing, and then the other person suddenly says, "Yeah, me too!" Now we've been validated in how we feel, and we don't feel so alone anymore because there's somebody else going through the same things that we're going through. Talking to my colleagues or friends always lowers my anxiety.

The next benefit of having strong relationships is having a longer lifespan. It surprised me when I was gathering content for my original Super Chicken presentation about how loneliness threatens our longevity more than obesity and smoking. This makes sense because relationships give us a certain sense of purpose and, as we just talked about, boost our mood and are great for our mental health.

Another benefit of building relationships is simply your quality of life. When we have friends, we tend to make plans with them. We might plan to go out for a hike, supper, or take a class together. Of course, I want to share a story with you about this.

New and Exciting Adventures
You already know that I live in a tiny home and live near the top of a mountain. I live in a campground where there are twelve pads to rent. I recently developed a new relationship with a lady that lives here with her husband, two lovely children, and a precious little pup. At the time of writing this, it is summer, the weather has been amazing, and we have had some opportunities to do things we both enjoy together. We have gone on some hikes together, tried out a

great Mexican restaurant (which she had been to before), and found a fantastic place to paddleboard with many unique treasures. We recently went out on the ocean, in a bay, and found thousands of sand dollars (both alive and not), hundreds of baby jellyfish, and so many different shells that were just beautiful. I wouldn't have gone to this spot without her suggesting it and showing it to me. It's my new favourite place.

We also planned a three-day trip up island where I found the biggest and most amazing jellyfish, did a full day paddle in an inlet, saw tons of starfish and sea anemones on the rocks around the islands, and went on an intense hike that brought us to some waterfalls where the salmon were spawning. We had fresh salmon and crab, gifted to us by the hosts of the VRBO we rented, right on the ocean. If I hadn't invested in this relationship, I would have missed out on something fantastic that helped make this summer the best I have ever had!

It's always fun to enjoy those things with somebody else, even though sometimes it's awesome to do it ourselves as part of our self-care routine. If we don't have those relationships, it might be easier to sit on the couch and binge-watch on Netflix, do a little bit too much snacking, and ruminate over something at work or in our personal lives. Having those relationships and having somebody to do things with might encourage us to be more active and in turn, improve our quality of life.

More on Core Strengths
I do a lot of team-building workshops using the Core Strengths assessments. Sometimes when folks ask me what

I do, I tell them I teach people how to build relationships. I want to share more about Core Strengths with you now to give those unfamiliar with it a better idea of what it is and why it is so valuable.

When I do an assessment with my clients, they immediately get their results, and the first thing that comes up is their motivational values system (MVS). To explain quickly, there are seven regions on this triangle that folks fall under. Folks are motivated by one of three things: people, performance, or process. We all have a blend of these three values, but one is usually higher than the other two. Blue represents those who value people more, always ensuring everyone is included and happy. Red represents those who value performance more; they are the ones who get things done, the movers and the shakers. And green represents those more focused on process, gathering information and making sense of things. Sometimes people have an MVS where all three of those are close, and they end up in the middle of the triangle called the hub. Those people are usually very flexible and adaptable. And then, of course, there are those regions where two values are close in ranking, red/green, red/blue, and blue/green.

This is one tool that I use to help organizations realize what motivates their team. In Chapter Three, when I talked about competition, I suggested identifying the strengths of the individuals in your organization. Discovering folk's strengths is another outcome of using this tool. In the Core Strengths assessment, we all have the same twenty-eight strengths to draw from, but we each use those strengths differently. These are shown to us in a strengths portrait, which is a diamond shaped diagram that indicates which strengths we tend to use the most at work.

The top strengths I use the most in my career are self-confident, quick-to-act, persevering, sociable, methodical, and ambitious. These strengths bring me the best results when used at work, facilitating my workshops, mentoring, or coaching a client. The ones I rarely use and avoid almost at all costs are modest (those who know me always laugh at that), analytical, and cautious. Being that those strengths are at the bottom of my strengths portrait does not mean I'm not good at them; they simply don't bring me the same successful results as using those at the top of my portrait.

Increasing Relationship Intelligence

The first step in increasing relationship intelligence is to have strong self-awareness and then to understand what motivates each member of your team, how they deal with conflict, what their strengths are, and how to communicate with them effectively. Once you have that knowledge, it's all about using that information to grow those relationships.

Self-awareness is yet another journey. The more you learn about yourself, the more questions you may have. It has certainly been interesting hitting that fabulous fifty mark and spending so much more time taking stock of who I am, what I'm doing, and where I spend my time. I love the self-discovery journey; if you aren't there yet, it's something to look forward to (pinky promise).

Self-awareness takes both time and energy. For example, if some opposition or a slight conflict happens at work, it takes time to take a step back and consider the following: what happened, what part did you play in it, how you could do things differently in the future, and what the plan could be moving forward. Often when we take the time to consider those questions, we learn something about ourselves. One of the key lessons I have learnt about conflict is that often, the conflict may have nothing to do with me.

For example, if a colleague comes into the office one day and bites someone's head off as soon as they enter the door, is it possible that something happened before they even left home that has nothing to do with you or work? Perhaps their partner reminded them they had to pick up the kids at four thirty p.m. from an after-school activity, which they forgot about, and scheduled a last-minute meeting. Now they must figure out either how to get the kids home or how to reschedule the meeting. Maybe this is embarrassing for them as they previously had to reschedule that same meeting and were criticized for it. This situation may put them on the edge, resulting in them being a bit cranky.

I highly recommend journaling as a self-awareness tool. I have had many self-realizations while journaling. I journal almost every morning and have done so for many years. I use this time to plan out my day, recap the previous day, make to-do lists, or sometimes use it to self-coach when I have an issue to deal with. Journaling, similar to other practices that bring about self-awareness, takes time that you have to carve out of your day somewhere. It needs to become a priority. I believe my many years of journaling even helped me write this book.

Reading is another way to increase your self-awareness. So many great authors have incredible books on self-awareness and self-improvement. There are many opportunities to participate in personal or professional development workshops or training through your organization, community, or other groups you are a part of. Have conversations with those around you to discover the opportunities that are available to you.

Another way to increase relationship intelligence is to practice active listening. We have talked about active listening in other chapters, which shows how important it is in all areas of organizational effectiveness. When we actively listen to our colleagues, friends, family, and acquaintances, we will understand them better, show them more empathy, and grow ourselves. When you listen to understand, you pay attention without interrupting, maintain eye contact (I respect that this is not something all cultures practice), and ask clarifying questions to confirm you understand what your colleague is trying to convey.

In all my years working with folks, I have learnt that if you have a relationship with them and know a bit about them personally, it is much easier to empathize with and support them. None of us know everything about what is going on in others' lives. We all have our own stuff. There are so many things we all must deal with, sometimes daily. These things could include financial, health, or relationship issues, or something totally different. Maybe our stress load is high, or the kids are getting into trouble in school, or our partner lost their employment, or for many of us who don't have a partner, at times, it may be challenging simply to make ends meet. By building our relationship intelligence and knowing those around us on a larger scale, we will be able to do what is needed to bring out the best in them (and ourselves) which is what we will explore next.

Hen House Highlights

- There is not one person who can fulfill every-thing that we need in just one relationship.
- Relationships can boost our mental health, lengthen our lifespan, and improve our quality of life.
- You can increase your self-awareness by completing personality assessments, jour-naling, reading, and active listening.
- When we actively listen to our colleagues, friends, family, and acquaintances, we will understand them better, show them more empathy, and grow ourselves.

CHAPTER 9

Bringing Out the Best in Yourself and Others

You've made it to the last chapter! And in my opinion, this one is one of the most important ones. Up to this point, we have discussed the critical aspects that need to be in place for your folks to thrive in your organization. These include positivity, resilience, competition, team building, productivity, community, psychological safety, and relationship intelligence. Once these aspects have been considered, implemented, and strengthened, folks can concentrate on being their best selves and bringing out the best in others. These two things go hand-in-hand.

Heffernan shared in her TED Talk that "bringing out the best in others is how they found the best in themselves." Let that sink in. Bringing out the best in others is how we find the best in ourselves.

> *We are being our best selves by supporting,*
> *encouraging, and collaborating with others.*

Bringing out the best in others is a key factor in successful organizations. The organization's culture needs to be one where everyone feels confident in their positions, where there is community and psychological safety, where strong relationships have been built, and where there is a certain camaraderie where everyone pitches in and helps others. Leadership needs to encourage this type of behaviour, and this can be accomplished first by those in charge when they model the way.

The Secret Cabin

Recently, I did something so far out of my wheelhouse, comfort zone, and ability, and I did it with two of my best friends. The mountain I live on has a hidden gem. There is a secret cabin about forty-five minutes up from the parking lot at the top of this mountain. I do some hiking, or what I thought was hiking, on the mountain. My idea of hiking is when I walk down the road two or three kilometres, then turn around and huff and puff my way back up. That's what hiking on the mountain is, right? Not at all!

I had heard about this secret cabin and thought it might be a fun adventure, so I reached out to a friend and asked her for directions, which she gave me. Around three p.m. on a hot Friday afternoon, my two friends and I decided to do this hike and try to find the secret cabin. We put on our hiking shoes, filled our water bottles, and set off on an adventure, knowing that even if we didn't find the cabin, we would have gotten some great exercise and probably seen some great views.

When we started, it seemed alright, not too challenging or steep. We made a pact that we would not be in a rush and would stop as often as needed to catch our breath—and for me, that was often. Our directions were to hike up the mountain for about a half hour, and that's when we would veer off the path we were on and head more into the woods. That half hour took forty-five minutes because of the stops, but remember, we weren't in a rush. The amazing part of the hike at that point was that every time we stopped to catch our breath, we would turn around to see where we had come from. The views were spectacular! We stood there in awe of the view and what we had already accomplished every time we rested. We took many pictures, but they didn't do the views justice. This hike was something you had to experience to get the full picture. It honestly took my breath away.

While climbing, we supported each other by offering ideas, such as holding on to tree branches to help us keep our balance in the steepest sections of the trail or suggesting different ways to navigate a tricky section. We talked about how for two of us, this was something we would have never done and that we were doing it now because of each other and the support we provided. We were being gentle, kind, empathetic, supportive, and understanding towards ourselves and each other—we were bringing out the best in ourselves.

We kept following the directions, which said: *You'll get to another clearing, walk to the left for a minute or two, and then the cabin is in the woods on the right-hand side, two-or three-minutes' walk into the woods.* There are no signs or markers, so we had to blindly trust the directions, hoping we took the right turns and the proper paths along the way. When, finally, I spotted the roof of the secret cabin in the woods, I was elated! I was so excited that we had found the cabin. The exhaustion from the hike disappeared like magic the minute I spotted it, and I felt so full of life. We had made it, and it was exhilarating!

We spent some time looking around both inside and outside the cabin. There was an outhouse, which was con-venient (you don't have to worry about how much water to use in the flush in an outhouse, FYI). On the deck were three lawn chairs where we took a break. Inside the cabin were dishes and silverware, frying pans and a colander, two chairs and a sofa, a set of bunk beds, a wood fire stove, some wood, brooms, slippers, hot chocolate, tang, and much more. It was stocked enough that anyone who decided to venture out could enjoy the final spot and even spend the night if they wanted. This hike was something I had never experienced before. Not only was it exhilarat-ing, it was exhausting as it was quite steep in places with shale-like rock, which made it unstable in those spots. But once we found the cabin, the only thing the hike was, was remarkable.

Coming back down the mountain was very challenging. Going up was a cardio workout, but going down on the shale path was steep and tricky. At times, to me, it felt dan-gerous. (I realize I have a greater fear of falling since I fell and broke my wrist.)

A lot of adrenaline was pumping through my veins during the descent. It was almost scary. There were times when we were all three standing in different places, trying to figure out the safest way to proceed. We kept encouraging each other, giving each other advice on what was working for us, and acknowledging how magnificent this adventure was and what we were accomplishing together.

Ultimately, it took us about two and a half hours to complete the hike. We only had one fall, which was as slow and graceful as possible; in fact, the two of us who didn't fall gave it a ten out of ten for structure and control. (It always helps to lighten up situations by making jokes.) My knees burned for the last hundred feet or so, and I thought I would be sore. Surprisingly, that didn't happen; the adrenaline and the massive accomplishment made the challenge and pain disappear. I will point out that after another three days of adventures and exploring, the adrenaline wore off, my friends went home, and I could barely walk for two days. Was it worth it? Hell yes!

This hike was one of my most significant mental and physical accomplishments and one that I am very proud of. It was scary, and I felt vulnerable. Through the challenge of making it to the top and back down, we strengthened our relationship and built our self-confidence. Will I do it again? I doubt it. Now that I know what the hike entails, I might have to pass. But I am glad we encouraged each other to try, keep going, and acknowledged how awesome we did. It is one of my favourite memories ever. We brought out the best in ourselves as well as in each other.

How to Promote Bringing Out the Best in Others
I previously shared that in the Super Chickens TED Talk, Heffernan said that what mattered was the mortar, not the

bricks? She said it's what holds the team together—the trust, the relationships, the empathy, the collaboration. When a team has all of that, they collaborate and bring out the best in others, and everyone shines; there are no super-stars or super chickens. Imagine being part of a team like that. How much fun would that be?

When the folks in your organization feel safe and secure, it is much easier to help others by lifting them up and sup-porting them. This result is something that happens over time. One must be diligent about promoting this type of culture and work at it daily. There is so much one can do to create this kind of environment. One absolute must is promoting psychological safety, which we explored in Chapter Seven, so that folks know it's okay to make a mistake, especially when trying something new. One could even encourage mistakes! Mistakes mean you are trying; trying something new, trying to stretch, trying to do and be better. What a great culture to have in your organization. You could even have a "best mistakes board" in your lunch-room, where you celebrate mistakes that your team makes when trying to grow and do better. It's all in the mindset. Mistakes equal opportunities to grow.

We discussed competition in Chapter Three and decided it is good when it is healthy. You can compete and bring out the best in others. In that chapter, I shared with you how Braeden and I encouraged and supported each other, even when competing, because—honestly—we wanted each of us to succeed. And by helping each other, we absolutely helped ourselves. It was never desirable for us to annihilate each other. That would not have been fun.

Transparency is another way to promote a positive culture where everyone can be their best selves. For example, say someone leaves your organization. When we don't know what happened, we always make up our own story. Rarely is that made-up story the truth. It's unnecessary to share every detail with your employees of why someone left but share what you can so that there is no doubt or fear around employee turnover. Having secrets, or at least appearing to, doesn't go over well with your team. When folks don't know why someone left or was let go, and the culture is insecure, they go into survival mode, making it more of a look-after-yourself type of culture. And don't give your team that load of crap that *our organization is just a stepping stone for other employment opportunities.* No organization can thrive when there is constant turnover. By being honest and transparent with your employees, you allow them to be secure, be their best selves and bring out the best in others.

To promote being at your best, admit when you, as the leader, have screwed up. Admitting mistakes is a brilliant way to promote a safe and secure culture. When your employees see you make mistakes and own up to them, they know it will be safe for them to do the same. Fessing up to your mistakes is hard if you allow your ego to get in the way. And if you have an ego that gets in the way of doing this, it will be next to impossible to create this type of culture for your teams. Making mistakes is great because it does mean you are trying to grow and explore new things and ideas.

Another way to bring out the best in others is to know what others are best at. Defining others' strengths is what

I love about working with the Core Strengths assessments. Through the assessment tool, it is determined what it is that motivates your members. You can look at their motivational value system and top strengths to determine where they will most likely excel. For instance, if someone lands in the green region of the triangle (has a focus on process), has "analytical" as a top strength, and you need to gather data and create a report, this is the person you can likely count on to do it well for you. If you know this and play into that strength, you will be setting them up to bring out the best in themselves.

And finally, you could have weekly celebrations that include the whole team to encourage bringing out the best in others. Have individuals give their teammates kudos for the little and the big things. That could be as simple as recognizing someone who covered for a teammate when they were off sick. Or someone that took the time to help with a technical issue or some other type of challenge. Make sure everyone is recognized for something. Everyone has great gifts to offer the team; you need to know what those gifts are.

Self-Care

Self-care is imperative when we want to bring out the best in ourselves. Self-care is taking action to preserve or improve one's health. When I write that, it sounds pretty significant: *to improve one's health*. I don't know if many of us take it that seriously, but we should. Today's world is just so busy. We often try to do many things, be in many places, and solve many problems, sometimes all at once. By not practicing self-care, we might add to our problems.

There is a video where Oprah Winfrey talks about self-care. In this video, Winfrey (2014) says, "You don't have anything to give that you don't have." She also says your job is to work on yourself, fill yourself up, and keep your cup full. She shares that she used to fear that because of what people might think or say, perhaps thinking she is full of herself or self-centred, but now she embraces it, and fills her cup. She tells us that self-care is honouring ourselves and that the design and why we are here are big. Oprah says that taking care of yourself is your most important job. Only when you fill up your cup can you give to the rest of the world. Oprah's comments confirm that we must practice self-care to bring out the best in ourselves, and only then will it be possible to bring out the best in others.

There are so many ways we can practice self-care daily. We can go for a walk, be kind and do random acts of kindness, pay attention to what we are doing and what matters, set priorities, and eliminate things that are not important. We can be curious and explore new things and places, contribute more to our community, slow down and take a breath, and even journal or read a book. We can support others and ask for support, do things that spark joy or bring us pleasure, and accept what we have, where we are, what we can change, and what we cannot. These are all acts that promote self-care.

I created a presentation on self-care that was part of a personal development series I offered. When creating content, I found that research suggests that self-care promotes positive health outcomes, such as fostering resilience, living longer, and becoming better equipped to manage stress—not that many of us have stress in our lives (this is sarcasm in case you missed it).

Self-care is crucial. Without it, we get sick, run our energy levels down too low, and lose track of what we are doing and how we are living. Life is short, even when we take care of ourselves, but it can be much shorter when we practice very little or no self-care.

What self-care is to one person might be different than it is to another, and what you do today for self-care might be different than what you do tomorrow. It's all about what works for you and what you need physically, emotionally, mentally, and spiritually. And, of course, that can change several times during our lives based on what we are going through and experiencing.

The more often we practice self-care the more resilience we build and our whole spirit will be more vital. Again, there are several things you can practice daily. You can take time to relax, even if it's just for a quick ten-minute bubble bath (a half hour would be better). You can go outside, move, exercise, breathe fresh air, and feel the sunshine on your face. You can unplug, even if that is shutting your phone off thirty minutes before going to bed. All these things can be done daily.

Self-care is about many other things as well. It's about getting enough sleep and looking after your health (like regular doctors' appointments, massages, physiotherapy when necessary, etc.). It's about having a healthy diet, drinking enough water, and taking a break when you need some downtime.

A year and a half after I moved to Vancouver Island in British Columbia, I took up paddleboarding, and now it is my go-to for self-care. It is where I can get grounded, and I don't think about anything except being on the water and where the sea lions are. It's funny, but my breathing slows right down when I am out there. One time, I completely stopped breathing. Here's a story for you.

I See a Sea Lion

One autumn day, I decided to go out alone for a paddle. It was only my third time out, so I was still getting comfortable and learning the ropes. The salmon had started spawning and were very active, jumping all around me (which always makes me giggle). Folks were fly-fishing in the shallow waters (which is where I paddleboard for safety reasons and to be able to see all the amazing treasures on the ocean floor), and a few fishing boats sat stationary and were casting their hooks. I heard a noise I hadn't heard before; it was a huffing noise. I looked around and saw a sea lion looking at me from probably fifty feet away. I had never seen one on my board before and was uncomfortable, so I paddled away rather quickly.

A while later, after paddling along the shore, I realized I needed to start heading back, meaning I would have to return to where I had my first sea lion encounter. When I got back to that same spot, sure enough, the sea lion was still there, and so were the folks fishing. I stopped and watched as the sea lion bobbed its head up and down, disappeared for a few minutes, then came back up and looked at me again. After about ten minutes, the sea lion went down one last time and—surprisingly—swam right towards me.

Not only did she swim towards me, but she went right underneath my paddleboard! Now I call it she, as female sea lions are supposedly more curious than males, so the sea lion was likely female. I know my eyes were wide, and I had a look on my face, and when I looked up, there was a fisherman in a boat laughing his butt off at me. I asked him loudly and somewhat crazedly if I should be scared. He laughed and said he always dove with them, and that they were harmless. I will reserve that conclusion for a few more years until I have had more experience with them. I expect this is a once-in-a-lifetime thing, but we shall see. (It hasn't happened again in over thirty more times out paddleboarding.) What a thrilling experience! I will share that the next summer, the friend that I made who also lives up here on the mountain, with whom I have had many adventures, was out on her paddleboard alone, and a sea lion actually tried to climb onto her board! That is an experience I don't need to have. I love the sea lions so much that I recently got a tattoo of one, but I don't have any desire to share my paddleboard with one.

Everything, including my breathing, is easy when I am out on my board. Sometimes I'm only out there for half an hour, and other times, I stay there for three or four hours. It depends on what I find during my exploration. Sometimes I see starfish, jellyfish, seals, cool shells, other fish, crabs, and almost always, the sea lions. It's pure beauty and serenity, and it fills my soul.

It's crucial to find a space that is special for you. It could be in the woods, on a trail, in your boat, by a lake, in the bathtub, in your backyard, or you could create a special space in your house. You could have a favourite chair, a salt rock lamp, or some artwork that speaks to you. Maybe it's a sacred space to do yoga, read, meditate, do crafts, or just be. It may be a park, a museum, a gallery, or even a little coffee shop. This can be a place you go to just be present, take a break, or get grounded, and if you're lucky, perhaps all three. Remember, self-care is necessary when you want to bring out the best in yourself.

The Importance of Sleep, Exercise, and Food

Sleep is one of, if not the most, significant aspects of self-care. In 2005, the Agricultural Health and Safety Network in Saskatchewan created a video called Sleepless in Saskatchewan that resonated with me. The video focuses on farm families and sleep, but the content pertains to everyone.

In this forty-five-minute video, Jon Shearer, a sleep researcher, shares with us some things we can do to improve our sleep. These include having a white noise machine, keeping your bedroom three to five degrees cooler than the rest of the house, changing your sheets regularly (he suggests using 100% cotton sheets), having a great pillow, and making sure there is no light coming into your room. He says if you must have noise to fall asleep to, such as music or the TV, make sure it's on a timer. He also suggests getting a timer and having your bedside lamp come on a half hour before your alarm, limiting your caffeine and alcohol (especially three or four hours before bed), and exercising (again, at least three hours before bed). Jon also talks about taking a twenty-minute nap halfway through your work cycle, whether at night or during the day. Napping at work might be difficult in some organizations.

Shearer then goes on to share that when we don't get enough sleep, our mental health suffers, and our mood is affected. The video states that sleep deprivation puts us at higher risk for certain cancers, late-onset diabetes, fertility problems, stroke, congestive heart failure, high blood pressure, and the inability to absorb prescription drugs. Those are many great reasons to encourage us all to get a better night's sleep. After we take care of our sleep, I believe how we move our bodies and what we put into our bodies is the next important thing to consider.

Exercise is of utmost importance. It doesn't have to be massive, hard, take tons of time, or even cost you any money. You can find a YouTube video series on yoga, for example. The one I follow is with Melissa West and only takes ten minutes daily. I do it just before I start work in the morning. You can go for a walk, a hike, get on a bicycle, go fishing, go for a swim, play in your garden or flower bed, or so many other things that cost little or no money.

The other thing we need to be aware of is what we put into our bodies and try to make good choices. Some foods, such as fatty fish, blueberries, nuts, leafy greens, legumes, and veggies like broccoli and Brussels sprouts promote better health. Changing how you eat can improve your health and give you more energy to move and do the things you enjoy. Again, we do better if we limit our caffeine and alcohol, especially at night.

Practicing self-care takes a lot of energy, planning, and time, so you need to do certain things to help you succeed. For instance, one of the things you can do is learn how to say no and make more time for yourself. We all have friends, colleagues, and family members who regularly request our time and energy. It's great to say yes when you can, but this doesn't have to be every time someone asks. If you're already stressed and tired, overworked, and over-committed, you need to find a way to take back some of your time and save space for your own self-care. If you don't protect your energy and time, it can lead to burnout, anxiety, and irritability. By saying no, you build your confidence and resilience and give yourself more time to care for what is most important: you!

We all need breaks occasionally, whether that be for a day, a weekend, or a mini vacation. Taking breaks doesn't have to be expensive, either. You can even plan a staycation, do something special, something different. You could go somewhere you've never been. That could be simple, like a park, trail, museum, or whatever place that will help fill your soul. A staycation self-care weekend could look like eating delicious healthy meals, exploring something new, or just taking a nap or a bubble bath. Maybe you used to paint or draw and want to take that up again. You could grab your sketchbook and head to a river, a park, or somewhere that will inspire you. If you aren't sure what that looks like for you, just close your eyes and think about where you feel most alive or remember something you used to do that sparks joy in you, that activity can point you in the right direction.

If you enjoy reading, that can be an excellent activity for self-care. You can choose a book that takes you on an adventure and gives you a bit of a break from what is sometimes a hectic life. You could also read a book on self-care to learn about other activities or ideas to honour yourself and take better care of yourself. If you don't like reading, you could always listen to a book, podcast, or watch a video on YouTube. There are lots of options to learn, grow, and take better care of yourself.

> *Self-care is pertinent to bringing out the best in you and the best in others, both at work and outside of work.*

If you are an employer or a leader, support the idea of self-care, as it will only benefit you in the long run. If you encourage your employees to take care of themselves, you will deal with less absenteeism, burnout, and turnover. Your team will be in tip-top shape and be more effective, productive, and creative at work.

Bringing out the best in yourselves and others is a great practice, not only for organizational effectiveness but also for personal growth. Self-care is one of the most important things you can do to thrive both in your career and in your personal life. Pay attention to how well you sleep, how much you move, and what you put into your body. Do what best honours your body, and your body will do the best for you.

Hen House Highlights

- Bringing out the best in others is how we find the best in ourselves.
- Mistakes equal opportunities to grow.
- Research suggests that self-care promotes positive health outcomes, such as fostering resilience, living longer, and managing stress better.
- Sleep is one of, if not the most, significant and most important aspects of self-care.

Conclusion

C ongratulations! You made it to the end of the book. Seeing you made it this far, I hope you have found value in what you read. I enjoyed putting the information together for you.

So, what did we learn from this book? We learnt that:

- Being a super chicken is not all it's cracked up to be (my attempt at humour).
- We best perform when we are part of a team with high empathy, inclusion, and diversity.
- We explored the themes found in Heffernan's video, including positivity, resilience, competition, team building, productivity, community, psychological safety, relationship intelligence, and being our best selves and bringing out the best in others.

In May of 2023, I offered my colleagues the Super Chickens presentation virtually. In fact, I have offered this presentation on three occasions, so far. I always leave time at the end for questions or discussion. One of the folks on the call had a fascinating question. He asked, "If we need to stop being super chickens, what kind of chickens should we be?" Brilliant. I didn't know the answer then, but I took a stab at it. I suggested we need to be inclusive chickens. I don't think that's the exact answer though. We may need to be compassionate, positive, loving chickens or all of the above. What I know for sure is we need to be chickens that understand the importance of building relationships with others and how that improves our life and well-being.

Another thing I know at this point in my journey is we need to have very strong self-awareness to lead in this world. We need to better understand ourselves and the folks we interact with. We must listen to understand and eliminate the judgment we frequently carry. People are usually doing the best they can with what they have. Hopefully, we can honour them and give them credit for that.

Seldom do we know the whole story. We should acknowledge and accept that. There is so much more going on, or that has happened than we might know. We need to take a step back and consider what we don't know about the story or the situation before choosing how we proceed. We need to have an open heart and lead with love. So, what kind of chicken is that? Is that an enlightened chicken? Does that type of chicken even exist? One that is full of love, has no judgement, and is self-aware? It's complicated.

When pondering further, I think of my thesis supervisor from my master's degree. To me, he is the answer. He is full of love, acceptance, and understanding, with absolutely no judgment. He is quirky and wears such cool hats. He kind of looks like the nutty professor and is comfortable in his own skin. I adored him so much that I named my youngest Dachshund after him. They are both of German descent, so smart, and full of love (I know I already said that, but it is both their best qualities and needs to be repeated). Their name is Niels. When thinking of him (the man, not the dog), some words that come to mind are authentic, loving, accepting, encouraging, inclusive, understanding, selfless, and curious. I am still searching for the answer to what kind of chicken we need to be and these are the qualities I think are most pertinent.

As they say in show business, "That's a wrap." Again, I hope you have found value in the content contained in these chapters. I also hope you have found one or two helpful nuggets to take away. And finally, I hope that it is more than just using more water when you flush a camper toilet. In any event, I know many of you will be reminded of this book when you do flush, and for that, I am grateful.

About the Author

In 2020, Lana T. Bavle, founder of LTB Leadership, moved from small town Saskatchewan to Vancouver Island to fulfill her dream of living in a tiny home surrounded by rainforest on the Pacific Ocean.

As she downsized her life to fit into her new humble abode, she adopted the mantra of living tiny, thinking big, and creating balance. In 2020, Bavle officially left her career in Municipal Government to pursue her passion of helping others through leadership development, team building, and coaching via LTB Leadership.

Bavle completed her Master of Arts in Leadership along with her Certificate in Executive Coaching at Royal Roads University in Victoria, BC. She is a certified facilitator for the Core Strengths SDI Assessments and works as an educator to help you take simple steps each day that will move you closer to your personal dreams. With over fifteen years of experience working in Municipal Government as CAO, Bavle's experience and education offer a truly unique set of resources.

She now operates LTB Leadership from her tiny home, affectionately named "The Hummingbird," and finds balance in her life through paddleboarding, beach combing, going on adventures (taking photos of said adventures), and going for long walks on the beach with her two wiener dogs.

With Gratitude

To start, I wish to thank Vern and Hayley Sabeski for lighting that flame and encouraging me to write this book. It's been fun to share all the stages with you and I don't know how long it would have been before I would have decided to do this on my own. Your friendship is a treasure to me, and for that I am grateful.

Next, thanks to all my friends and colleagues for giving me the experiences that in turn gave me all these great stories to share. It has been a pleasure having you in my life and I am beyond grateful for your presence.

I have two amazing executive coaches I wish to thank: Alisa Harrison and Lynn Wark. While I was working on this book, the subject of the book itself became one of my coaching topics on many occasions. Having you both as my thinking partners gave me the courage and motivation to continue, and for that I am grateful.

Thank you to Twila Walkeden and Lynn Wark for peer reviewing my manuscript and giving me your feedback. I value your friendships and your input. You have made the content in this book more engaging for those who will read it. It was a nice little present, wrapped up in a box, and you put the ribbon and bow on it. I am so lucky to be able to call you my friends, and for that I am grateful.

And finally, I am grateful for the position of privilege I have that presented me with the opportunity to sit down and write this book. Life is so interesting and full of exciting opportunities to learn and grow. The universe, my upbringing, my education, my courage, and my persistence have given me great gifts, including this book, and for that I am forever grateful.

References

Bavle, Lana. *Improving the Leadership Capabilities of Municipal Elected Officials through Saskatchewan Association of Rural Municipalities.* Master's thesis, Royal Roads University, 2020. ProQuest (28027607).

Bishop, Kathy, Dr. (November 16, 2017.) *MA Leadership Program - Dr. Kathy Bishop, School of Leadership Studies,* video, 8:57. Victoria BC: Centre for Teaching and Educational Technologies, Royal Roads University. https://www.youtube.com/watch?v=seBiFAT4k6Q&t=12s.

Brown, Brené. (2012). *Daring Greatly.* New York, NY: Penguin Random House LLC.

Brown, Juanita, & Isaacs, David. (2005). *The world cafe: Shaping our futures through conversations that matter* (1st ed.). San Francisco, CA: Berrett-Koehler Publishers, Incorporated.

Cooperrider, David, & Whitney, Diana. (2005). *Appreciative Inquiry: A Positive Revolution in Change.* Oakland, CA: Berrett-Koehler Publishers.

Edmondson, Amy. (2019). *The Fearless Organization.* Hoboken, NJ: John Wiley & Sons, Inc.

Heffernan, Margaret. (June 16, 2015.) *Why it's time to forget the pecking order at work,* video, 15:47. Vancouver, B.C.: https://www.youtube.com/watch?v=baHr-8kTbws.

Jagoo, Krystal. (2022). *Social Connectedness is Essential Component Mental Health Intervention.* https://www.verywellmind.com/social-connectedness-essential-component-of-mental-health-intervention-5215382

Kouzes, James, & Posner, Barry (2017). *The leadership challenge: How to make extraordinary things happen in organizations.* Hoboken, NJ: John Wiley & Sons, Inc.

Stabler, Lorna, Maura MacPhee, Benjamin Collins, Simon Carroll, Karen Davison,Vidhi Thakkar,Esme Fuller-Thomson, Shen (Lamson) Lin and Brandon Hey. (2021) "A Rapid Realist Review of Effective Mental Health Interventions for Individuals with Chronic Physical Health Conditions during the COVID-19 Pandemic Using a Systems-Level Mental Health Promotion Framework." *International Journal of Environmental Research and Public Health.* 18 (23), 12292. https://doi.org/10.3390/ijerph182312292

The Canadian Centre for Rural & Ag Health. (May 21, 2013) *Sleepless in Saskatchewan, Making Sleep Work for You,* video, 49:41. Saskatoon, SK.: https://www.youtube.com/watch?v=4DFJ-ZZh_Jg

Wagamese, Richard. (2016). *Embers.* Madeira Park, B.C.: Douglas and McIntyre (2013) Ltd.

Whitney, Diana, Trosten-Bloom, Amanda, & Rader, Kay. (2010). *Appreciative leadership.* New York, NY: McGraw Hill.

Winfrey, Oprah. (May 24, 2014.) *Stanford Graduate School of Business.* video, 3:18. Standford, CA.: https://youtu.be/kfLGR0KYuys